The Camden Poet

Irene Romilly
Poems of war, protest & peace

foreword by
Lady Roget - Romilly

THIS BOOK IS DEDICATED TO ALL THE CHILDREN AND PEOPLE IN THE WORLD, NOW TORN BY WARS, HUNGER AND IN-EQUALITY, HOMELESSNESS AND FEAR, IF ONLY, I, IN MY SHALL WAY, CAN PUT BACK THE SUN, MOON AND STARS IN THE SKY, AND TAKE AWAY THE HORROR AND DESTRUCTION, AND REPLACE IT WITH PEACE, PLENTY, AND EQUALITY.

Irene Romilly

Dedication from Irene Romilly's book of poems, *'Not Dead Yet'*
published 1984

For Irene's grandchildren; Cary, Sasha, Joby, Maj (Denmark), Nigel, Edwin, Jane, Clare (Yorkshire), child in Brazil? Great grandchildren; Honey, Harley, Ted and Jonas (Denmark) others Yorkshire/Brazil? Also with thanks to; Honey Simmonds, Cary Simmonds, Victorine Martineau, Andy Barklem and Mimi Romilly

The Camden Town Poet, poems of war protest & peace

First Edition: Published November 2014

Barklem Print & Publishing

166 Archway Road

LONDON

N6 5BB

U.K.

ISBN: 978-0-9551162-2-3

Publication Copyright © 2014 Barklem Print & Publishing: andy@barklem.com

All rights reserved: This book may not be reproduced in whole or in part, in any form or by any means, electronic or mechanical, including photocopying and recording, or by any information storage and retrieval system, without permission in writing from the publisher.

Poems by Irene Romilly: Copyright Estate of Irene Romilly © 2014

Contents:

"There's nothing more wonderful than being alive and having enough to survive"
Irene Romilly

Irene Romilly's entrance into the world coincided with her distant relatives going down with the Lusitania in May 1915. She herself managed to survive until 1994, she died aged 78, leaving hundreds of poems of war, protest and peace. Irene hated war, having been orphaned (aged 3) with her four sisters after her father, Private Frederick William Romilly – a soldier in the Royal Fusiliers during the First World War – died at Etaples, France, 6 days before the end of The Great War. Her mother died shortly afterwards, whereupon the children were all sent to Chase Farm Orphanage in Enfield, Irene was later sent to a convent in Swanage to train to go into service, from which she ran away to London in 1929 aged 14. At first she slept rough in Regents Park, (*The Flag of Peace pp117*), until she found a job and a room to live (*A Penny A Time pp6*) at 46, Camden Road, Camden Town.

Some of her poems reproduced here for the first time reflect the turblulence and upheaval many ordinary people experienced through the devastion brought about by the brutality of the first and second World wars. As a result many of the poems are anti-war; *Daddy Daddy, You Sent Them To Die* and *A 100 Year Secret's Act*. Whilst others are quite tender and poignant; *Moonbeams, No Place To Hide* and *I Wonder How They Came To Be There*. Some are still contemporary; *BP You Think You're Funny, You Can't Buy A River and The Protest*. They are compassionate; *Our World Is Here, The Price Of Life* and *My World*. There are also poems about politicians; *The Pinewood Box* and the economy; *A New Disease – Monopolies, Please Take It Away* and *The Bank Manager*. Others are about life in Camden; *At the Lock* and *I Hate Sundays* and championing the poor and down-and-out; *I Walk Around And I See* and *I Say Hello Then Sit Down And Cry*.

All the poems express a deep feeling of personal disenfranchisement of injustice inherent in society itself and the inequality and mythology that is propagated and upheld by the establishment. They are poems of a life of lonliness and loss, a direct result of the senseless murder and destruction of war. Irene combated this grief and trauma by recording her feelings, frustrations and hopes in a vernacular prosaic form which is often touching, sad but not without humour and sardonic wit. Irene, *The Camden Town Poet*, walked the streets, her memories are in the landscape, the landscapes are in you. The poem *Take Me, Take Me*, is about a bomb that landed in King's Cross during the Second World War (see Irene's account of this event *ppx and pp159*) it recounts the death by slow gassing of an innocent family.

Her first book of poems *'Not Dead Yet'* was published in 1984 and she had poems published in the St. Pancras Chronicle, the Camden New Journal and the Evening Standard.

Irene spent most of her life in Camden Town, the last 30 years living at 109a Camden Street, just around the corner from where she first arrived in 1929. Irene didn't know that she shared this neighbourhood with her ancestors and that she had literally and unwittingly followed in their footsteps, for most of her life.

She once noticed that there was a hat shop in Camden High Street (next door to the tube station) called Romilly's, but she had no idea that it was owned – along with another shop in Mayfair – by Nellie Romilly, sister of Clementine Churchill and was financed by Churchill himself.

Nellie and Colonel Bertram Romilly's two anti-fascist sons, Esmond Romilly, who married Jessica Mitford, fought in the Spanish Civil War, had knuckleduster fights with the fascists in the East End and was involved with a communist bookshop in Camden. Giles Romilly who, as the nephew of Sir Winston Churchill was incarcerated in Colditz during WW2, were distantly related to Irene, all being descendants of Sir Samuel Romilly.

Irene was quite unaware of her illustrious ancestors; Sir Samuel Romilly, (1757-1818), Peter Mark Roget (1779-1869, of Thesaurus fame) and Sir William Job Collins (1859-1946) all interrelated of Huguenot descent and all Camden residents. Sir Samuel Romilly, a barrister and MP (known as *The Friend of the Oppressed*), was a pioneer of the abolishment of capital punishment, worked alongside Wilberforce in the early stages of the anti-slavery campaign. Sir Samuel lived at 27 Gower Street and at 21 Russell Square and had chambers at Grays Inn and Lincolns Inn.

Sir Samuel's nephew, Peter Mark Roget (as well as starting on his thesaurus at the age of seventy) is given credit in Hollywood for his pioneering contribution to the advancement of the film industry, after his paper on *The Persistence of Vision*, was published by The Royal Society in 1824. He worked on several inventions including an early frigidarium with Jeremy Bentham, contributed greatly to the Encyclopaedia Britannica. As a physician he worked at the Northern Dispensary which was formerly in Euston Road and held a clinic for the poor in Somers Town, at 9 Somers Place. Roget lived in the house that Sir Samuel had purchased for him, at 39 Bernard Street, Bloomsbury.

There was an interesting incident that occurred in Camden High Street on New Year's Eve 1800; Roget had been invited to a New Year's Eve ball, held by the Romilly's in Pratt Place (situated on the right-hand side of the High Street going north from Mornington Crescent). It must have been quite a big event as he had to book lodgings nearby, but due to returning so late after the ball, he was locked out in the freezing snow for quite sometime.

Sir William Job Collins (related through Sir Samuel Romilly's mother's family, the Garnault's) was an ophthalmic surgeon, MP for St. Pancras and lived at 1 Albert Terrace,

Primrose Hill. His father owned pharmacies in Camden High Street and Parkway, as a doctor he was present at the first anaesthetic given in England in 1846, at 24 Gower Street.

Sir William was responsible for establishing the London Ambulance Service and also founded the former polytechnic in Prince of Wales Road. The Regents High School in Somers Town, was formerly named after him, his wife was Matron at the Temperance Hospital, in Hamstead Road, for many years.

Irene had many family members who had lived in Camden before her over the last 250-300 years which also included the Garnault's, who were treasurers, directors and major shareholders of the *New River Company* (the lynchpin of the above Huguenot descendants). The company had several reservoirs in Camden, including one at Tolmers Square (where the Tolmer cinema was later situated and where Irene had lived). Sir Samuel Romilly's brother, Thomas Romilly, lived nearby at 71, Warren Street. There was a director of the Bank of England, MP and Lord Mayor of London (1761) Sir Samuel Fludyer, Bt (1704-1768) and Thomas Walsh, the Georgian cartographer who lived in Chalton Street and Clarendon Square, Somers Town in 1800 and at various addresses in King's Cross (interestingly, he engraved a contour map of London for Robert Mylne of the *New River Company*). His daughter Evelina Baker, (Irene's great-grandmother) married at the Old St. Pancras Church, Pancras Road.

Irene met her Indian partner through the racing tipster *Prince Monolulu*, Irene and her partner (who worked for Doctor Bhattacharyya, at 122 King's Cross Road, where many of the tiny community of Indians often went at that time) lived in King's Cross, with their two young sons (mixed race relationships were frowned upon and extremely unusual at that time). Later, her partner ran off with another woman, taking her two sons with him, after which she met and eventually had a daughter with a student barrister whose chambers were at 9, Kings Bench Walk, who is now honoured with a plaque at his former home at 33, Tavistock Square. Nevertheless, she promptly left him several years afterwards after finding out where her two sons were and kidnapping them back. Taking her three children with her from Tavistock Square to the slums of Somers Town, she struggled stoically to bring them up by herself, working night and day (see her account about the film stars David Niven et al, whom she befriended as a hotel night telephonist ppxii). She had no help whatsoever from their fathers, living only for her children and unbelievably, considering her leftist leanings, she sent her children, on and off, to private schools (her eldest son became a professor of mathematics and a university lecturer). Irene had an extremely hard life was always poor and consequently many of her hardships are reflected in her poems and her longing for peace and justice in the world.

Irene's name means *'peace'*

Excerpt from a transcription of Irene's written account of the King's Cross bomb, Argyle Street, circa 1940

...sounded, my husband rushed with Nicholas... ...shelter in the basement, taking toys and pillows... ...was not there. I had gone to the fish and chip shop... ...they kept open, until bombed three months later, and... ...there, and she was telling me that she had her... ...two daughters, the sons were in the army, navy and... ...were the girls, and had come home for a reunion... ...and not enough food to feed them, went out to get some fish and chips, so happily. We held up until the all-clear siren sounded, and then rushed back home. A state of indescribable horror met our eyes, as disbelievingly we gazed at what was once a road. The Jerries had evidently tried to hit King's Cross station, but as it was camouflaged, they missed and hit the street opposite. Fortunately, they missed the house where my husband and son were in the basement. It was then that I gave up all pretence of being religious, and in one short moment became an atheist, everything I had heard, about the English and Germans, and everyone who wreaks violence upon the innocent. The lady who, was a proud mother, and had been talking about her lovely children, rushed past me screaming, and her hair turned literally white. The houses appeared outwardly alright, except for a pile of rubble, but the bomb had hit the gas mains and the people would have been alright, if they had not gone down to the Andersen Shelters, for the gas escaped, and they died before they could get out, or help came. But the worst thing that happened was at the pub next door to us. There were three little children, ages ranging from one to five years, and they ran down to the Andersen directly they heard the siren, and the parents were just going to follow when the bomb dropped, and the children were trapped. Well, those children never came out alive, the Air Raid Warden and volunteers tried to rescue them for three days. As they tried to dig, the earth fell in, burying the children. To this day, I can hear those pitiful little cries, getting fainter and fainter every hour. I was so distraught, until at last, everybody was sobbing piteously, for there was just nothing we could do, but let them die. Oh I shall never forget that day.

Excerpt from a transcription of Irene's written account of life in King's Cross during the Second World War

...or all the other ensuing days, when it... ...apathetic, incredulous fellows, that we were... ...position of self-preservation. Then came 1940 ....when the air raid sirens sounded, and the enemy...the horizon, taking flasks filled with tea, coffee...pillows and various other things, for we did not... ...We left our houses, whether we would ever return... ...uncertain. I gradually came to the conclusion that... ...was to the country for safety, I could no longer work... ...and night, my mind was possessed with fear, as were the fears of not only myself but every parent, and in fact, everybody in this war-torn country.

I am afraid, we were completely and utterly selfish, as the thought of all the mothers in the world, Germans, Jews, in fact, every human being in the world, whose love for their children was universal, and self-protective. May the powers that be, please forgive our apparent lack of humanity, as it was really beyond our comprehension at that time. To get back to the immediate issue which was to save the children, we prepared to evacuate them to places like Northampton, Bedford, Devon and Cornwall, which did not have any strategic value, in the military sense, so there was not so much danger of bombs dropping, and also I think, we had a very good barrage system, which we firmly believed would dissuade the enemy from entering the heart of Britain. How stupid we were, for their destruction was most thorough. I then had moved to Regent Square, which was around the corner to the tragic street I described earlier, and managed to obtain a nice flat in the basement, and outside in the garden was an Andersen Shelter, not, fortunately, under the building, and when the siren went, we either went there or the church, the King's Cross Tube station, or the underground shelter in the gardens in the square, which had been completely made into a shelter, underneath the whole space, and everything was to hand, a kitchen, bunks, and a room for adults and children to sleep separately, if they wished. They played cards, radios etc, and tried generally to forget the holocaust which was becoming a daily companion and lasted for another five long years. The apathy grew, and also the latent instincts of kindness also grew, we became very solicitous toward each other, worrying about other people, which...

Excerpt from a transcription of Irene's written account of the racing tipster, Prince Monolulu, often seen in films from the 1940's-50's

I only worked five nights a week so had weekends free, I was able to go out. This, by the way, was only in the summer. In the winter, I just hibernated, and to all intents and purposes just died, to come back to life with the sun. I met an African who, I found out later, went under the name of "I Gotta Horse". There was no involvement of any kind, he was, like me, living in a bedsitter, furnished very sparsely. It was situated in Cleveland Street right opposite the Post Office Tower, that was built some two or more years before the time of which I write. He knew that I and others, did not really have much to eat, himself included and used to make curry and rice in great quantities in his room and about ten girls and boys, mostly around my age, used to congregate and also contributed as much as we could towards the cost. I can't say I was terribly enamoured by the diet, but at least we were spared the pangs of hunger and so life went on and discontent filled the land, the poor became poorer and we could either not see, or refused to see, perhaps, thro' plain apathy, or even a stupid sense of bowing down to our rulers, we, figuratively speaking, licked their boots and now, this is what we are doing. Slavery was rampant, tho' not under that name, it was called patriotism and love of country, call it what you will, but it was the thin edge of the wedge.

Excerpt from a transcription of Irene's written account of the film stars David Niven, James Robertson Justice and Maurice Chevalier

For a long time since, in fact, my dear friends James Robertson Justice and Maurice Chevalier now followed by another of the gang of three, David Niven, has passed away, and when I say, that the reason I called them that, was because way back in the 1960s, I worked for years at well known hotels, as a night telephonist, the Connaught, Savoy, Ritz, Berkeley, British Transport. It was at the Connaught that the three I mentioned before, stayed, and naturally they quite often used to talk to me, and sometimes took me into their confidence, and as I was a grandmother, James especially, would talk to me for hours on end, it was not so busy then, as it became more recently. The tragic life of this wonderful man, not many people will know about, but my heart went out to him, when, after I was telling him about my lovely grandchildren, four of whom live in Harrogate, one in London, and one born in Denmark, I have never seen, not even to this day, he broke down and cried. I'll never forget as he told me about his little son, who had drowned, he never forgot, neither did I. There was I, with three lovely children and six grandchildren, whom I couldn't even afford to buy treats for. In the past, I used to carefully wrap up the food I was given at work and take it home for my children and always found it difficult to survive, even though I had an office job during the day, as well as my night job, but I think James and also David Niven and maybe Maurice Chevalier understood, for every few weeks, they would slip a fiver in an envelope and leave it in the porter's desk. How grateful I was, they'll never know. Now, the three have gone, but I think we should wake up to the living, for the dead have gone and no way can we bring them back, I believe in the living, my life is dedicated to them.

A 100 years secret's act

Now it's sixty nine years out of a hundred when
Many many millions of our poor men
Were killed and today no one knows
Where their bodies went only near to where the poppy grows
It was a place in France hush hush and there
The most horrific things went on I declare
Under age camps for the boys
Atrocities and no toys
And all the things that they said
Wicked Germans and others all long dead
We're supposed to have done to millions of men
Not only ours but those beyond our ken
And I don't hear anyone demanding an enquiry here
And I ask and ask every day month and year
Say where is my dad and all the others too
What oh what did our rulers do
After all why do you want to hide
All the details or take us for a ride
If as you say you have our welfare at heart
A very strange way to behave for a start
Still I want to go to visit my dad's grave
And also try to bring to the public gaze
How we and our forefathers have been made
Patsies and scapegoats just to save
The lords and peers for whom so much our men gave

1983

A fine art

Please don't love me too much
For I'm afraid I'll get out of touch
I look at you and see beautiful eyes
As I vainly try to tell those lies
I've perfected to such a fine art
To hide the pain that's in my heart
So please don't love me too much
For I will miss your gentle touch
If I hurt myself I'll hear you cry
I cannot bear to see a tear in your eye
Or how to explain how I'll be
Able to tell you and make you see
Going away to live with the clouds
Looking down to see you in the crowds
So don't be sad when you see me no more
For I will be going to a farther shore
Where all the beauty of your little heart
Is perfected like the treasure of a fine art

A golden haze

I can see thro' a golden haze
Long long golden summer days
From the past so far away
I used to dream all the day
And even thro' the condemnation
The cruelty and aggravation
My hands are not raised to start
A war for there's peace in my heart
And as I sit alone and dream
Of faraway mountains and a stream
With sun and beauty everywhere
For everyone in the world to share
My heart is in a vast prism
As I try so hard to make a decision
For to no idol do I bow my head
Or change my mind from what I've said
As I look back on long summer days
Thro' a golden golden haze

A hung Parliament

We want a hung Parliament so they say
As long as we're all elected we'll get our pay
That's the most important thing to us anyway
Who cares if the people don't get their way

A new disease – monopolies

There's a new disease in the world today
It's not AIDS if you believe what I say
It's the monopolies and the banks
The terrorists who only go for lower ranks
The ones who have to pay for every single thing
Doesn't include the politicians or a king
As they talk about terrorists and killers I ask and say
What are they doing to billions every day
Exploiting the poor with markets galore
Lucky if we don't have to go to war

A penny a time

I sat in the gods for a penny a time
Watching the films of romance and crime
They tore at my heart I laughed and cried
The tears fell for those heroes who died
Al Jolson captivated my heart with his sad eyes
For hours I sat finding it hard to rise
And go back to my room where no one cared
Whether I was hungry cold or scared
Bread butter and cheese was the general diet
On Sundays I partook of a meal where it was quiet
In the room of my landlord for the sum of one shilling
They thought I was strange for I was unwilling
To talk to them or laugh just go back to my room
Where I had a gramophone and a record with the tune
Of *Red Sails in the Sunset* on one side and on the other
Blue Moon I wound it up and played one after another
As I waited for the weekend to come
So I could go back to that cinema and sit struck dumb
Watching those films of another life
Love songs and plenty of happiness and strife
Where I left behind all my tears and care
Laughing and crying and wishing I was there
Singing to myself *brother can you spare a dime*
All this for the sum of a penny a time
For now we've taken away all the gold from the sack
And those darling people will never come back
As the only ones now are soldiers' sons
With an unlimited supply of bombs and guns
And there are no more pennies and not even a dime
Now a pound takes the place of a penny a time

5.5.1978

A place called nowhere

The cats are meowing outside my door
I wonder why they keep coming for more
The poor things are hungry and filled with fear
At first they cringe as I come near
They do not know all I can give them is milk
And stroke their fur it feels like silk
I think how can I feed them as I did before
For prices are increasing and more and more
The plight of my people fills me with dread
How can I tell the poor cats as I stroke them on the head
I daren't let them in for that place in my heart
Is solely and exclusively set apart
For those who have nothing even the will
To fight back just wait and sit still
Waiting for a miracle to come to their aid
For they are so apathetic such a long cavalcade
Reaching from here to there and everywhere
And eventually perhaps to a place called nowhere
Oh I'll shut my ears to the cries of the stray
Cats and hope against hope they'll go away
For there is only a small place left for
Them not like it was in the past and before
When all I did was struggle to survive
To get to the top but all I did was dive
Down to the depths from a place called somewhere
To a place I'd forgotten and it's called nowhere
So that's why as I stroke their fur like silk
I can only give them a little of my milk
As they come back each day for more and more
And cry so loudly outside my door

9.4.1981

A thousand million thanks

A thousand million thanks to you
For all the little things you do
That show you really, really care
How I live, and how I fare
So a thousand million thanks to you
In actions you say, I love you
Your kindly, gentle, tender thought
When perhaps I'm overwrought
So I repeat again and again
As my tired, eager brain
Fills with pleasure, as I see your face
Wherever I look, it's in that place
A thousand million thanks to you
For the million things you do
And the tenderness you give
Making me want to live and live
For a million, million years
As you take away all my fears
And I feel the heavenly bliss
Of your loving, tender kiss
So a thousand million thanks to you
For the million things you do
In all the things that show you care
How I live and how I fare

24.12.1977

At the Lock

Prepare for all the eventualities such as the lower class bod
Who dares to want enough or can't contact god
And the old soldiers yes would you believe for it's true
Are still walking those streets and don't vote too
For the simple reason they have no homes or bed
They fought and lost limbs eyes and their head
Walk around plush buildings at the lock every day
Wondering how to get food they don't pray
Crawl into their cardboard boxes every night
Fought so those on the green belts can be alright
And enable a few idiots who can't see
That if it wasn't for all those now defunct they'd have ceased to be
They say we're making a Britain fit for the gods
But forget that those very ordinary bods
Do everything even the sewers and bring food from the ground
Build all those bunkers I hear are all around
Which incidentally I must remind all of you
Are there for the ones who always do
Make themselves top priority as they make hay
While others rot in filthy hovels just a stone's throw away

A thing called Profit and Loss

Persevere I've heard for years and I know
That was my forefathers motto long ago
Now after 10 years I know I'll never bow
Have come to the end don't want to know now
They tell our old how lucky they are
They've a roof over their heads can see a star
We'll let you relive all the wars too
Bring you back to the old times you knew
Let you dream in the dark of the days when you ran
Underground or away from the bombs and the gas, lived on bread and jam
Heard the cries of all those trapped and dying
Sobbed and sobbed and heard your kids crying
Looked to our monarchs for help and all we saw
Were the carriages as they waved and went past the door
And now we see the same luxury altho' they say
Petrol must go up and they must pay
Inflation has gone down oh goody two shoes
There are theatres and tourists and all the big do's
'Cos there's a thing called profit and no loss
Nine hundred and forty four billion oh gosh

A War to end all Wars in 1914

This they said, is the war to end all wars
Those same words have been repeated, and laws
Brought out to counteract, they say
All the evils of yesterday
And they all hide, hide their eyes
Close their ears and look at the skies
Buy land out of the weapons of misery and power
And say stupid things like *"Now is the hour"*

Big sister, big brother

Big sister big sister and big brother too
They're watching watching all of you
Don't forget, even when you sleep
They'll be counting statistics instead of sheep
Big sister big brother put your heads together
As you travel all over discussing whether
To buy missiles bombs guns ships and planes
Then look surprised at all the beauty and the strains
Of music played to laud you as you say
We want disarmament not tomorrow but today
But it's hard to believe a leopard can change
It's spots if you really mean what you said to exchange
The poverty and misery of the masses for peace
Good food and shelter, and to release
All humans from their bondage or do your best
Instead of just talking like all the rest
Big sister big brother we don't want you around
To dole out your goodies then harass us and hound
All we want is enough it's as good as a feast
We don't want to suffer or have the least
For our children are the salt and the flowers
Of the earth sea and sky so take away your powers
Stop watching and beating us with your spears
And the arrows of your scorn take away our fears
Then you won't need to watch or even go
All over telling everyone what they already know
And no one will be hungry cold or cry or pause
To wonder who's watching for the there'll be no cause

6.7.1987

BP – you think you're funny

BP, ha' ha' you think you're funny
As you take minerals in exchange for money
Dig the graves of all mankind
For uranium you will find
In those towns everywhere
Where pollution fills the air
Join the hands of south and west
North and east without rest
To bring the plague to all races
As you take us back a million paces

Windscale here, Rocksby Downs there
In southern Australia, everywhere
Their operations are the same
With companies like BP, what's in a name
Who gets fat and rich as cancer grows
You can bet your life, even the vulture knows

Ring out those bells in all of those towns
All converge on Rocksby Downs
Where BP have discovered uranium – black gold
Own and operate, and have sold
Leukaemia and horror as those who sit
In their counting houses, don't care a bit

Go to the lands where they say
No vultures fly anyway
And soon no people will be there
For BP and capitalism are everywhere
First the gold rush, then the gun
Now cancer, plutonium, uranium for everyone
And instead of Rocksby downs for the Aussies
It will be in all lands financed by the bosses

Get up, get up off your butts
Don't be puppets for the mutts
Or faceless objects passing by
As they process uranium into horror pie
BP want the earth and sky
Go all over the world, how they try
Ring out, ring out all the bells do
Shout about them leaking waste on you

How much does it cost for a gallon of oil
How much does it cost for them to spoil
A thousand million lives, as much as you buy
All you red blooded children, woman or guy
While companies like BP buy mines everywhere
Rocksby Downs, Windscale they don't care
Palaces, bunkers the stars and the moon
Will disappear with people if you dance to their tune
It is of course, a shining example
Of the uranium spoon we don't want to same

22.5.1985

Buckles ribbons and bows

You can remind me of all I've never had
And can tell me that I'm very very bad
But leave me my peace of mind
And leave the past far far behind
I do not care for silken clothes
Or for buckles ribbons and bows
All I want is the children's smiles
Laughter and kisses I'll walk for miles
As happiness echoes in their dancing feet
I can see that they get enough to eat
In spite of the ridicule in your voice
I don't want to have my own Rolls Royce
So you can keep your diamonds and your rings
As long as you leave me flowers and things
That cannot be bought to warm my heart
When I'm cold and my world falls apart
I hear your voice even in my sleep
It torments me and makes me weep
For I know you don't care for me
And I wish for wings so I can be free
Hovering around to see your warm
And guiding you to a safe port from the storm
So you can keep your love of diamonds and rings
For I do not want for any of those things
As all I need is in my baby's eyes
Transporting me to heaven and blue skies
So what use are gold and rings to me
For my riches cost nothing as you can see
The riches I have are completely free

Buy gas shares they say; *still on the make*

Buy gas shares blow you sky high
Don't wait till they reach the sky
All you lovely people the ones who can pay
We won't worry about those who have nothing no way
The Government are sitting on their butts
Buy buy buy all you silly mutts
If you can't afford a meter who cares
It's a moneymaking stunt they've had for years
And if you can't pay then we'll put you away
So wake up all you fools we'll get your pay
In the war we hid underground saw thousands killed by gas
Exploding underground and heard them say Mass
And pray for the souls they say they had when they were here
As we listen to the arguments for nuclear
But all that gas will be no good, for one day,
When those greedy locusts have had their way
And keep the buildings standing as they say
Radiation and missiles are not harmful anyway
For we know what gas, guns, bombs and germ warfare have done
For decades, and wonder what they have up their sleeves for everyone
As they make billions out of the wars they say we've won
And destroy all those lives, and block out the Sun

Celebrate that date

All over the world they'll celebrate soon
And all the old soldiers come out with a spoon
Tell of the tales of honour and war
Of the way they were heroes in the one before
And the blind and the maimed say you know the queen
Just like Victoria will be behind the scene
And they look at the streets that's if they can see
No arms or legs in wheelchairs but free
To exist as the ministers everywhere spout
Shout and grin as they go round about
Vote for us they say oh me oh my
That's if you want I say to die
Or come back without an arm or a leg
And stay alive by learning to beg
Just watch as the others worse off than you
Can even exist on a pittance too
And inside I scream as the children say
Mama what are they marching for today
And I turn away for my eyes
Can't even see the heavens and the skies
All I can hear is the top brass say
March away for your country today
And I feel so sick and tell them no way
For they're saving you for a worse fate to pay
As our beloved people stroll aimlessly around
No money no food and the falling pound
I want to shout and say why don't you hear
But they'll never listen that's perfectly clear

Current fashion

We hear so much what people say
Regarding the children of today
It seems we've heard it all before
In the days before the war
For as we pass along the street
They seem so small and so sweet
Back goes the mind to days of yore
And thoughts abound for evermore
Folk said when we were very young
We just laughed and sung and sung
And never behaved in such a funny way
Or so the older generation always say
Why is it so the memory fades
As time goes into the decades
And we forget in all sincerity the fact
That once we were all like that
So let us hope that one day soon
Folk will stop reaching for the moon
And think of humanity with compassion
Not just because descrying folk is the current fashion

Daddy, Daddy

Daddy daddy you didn't have time to dream
Before they took you to fight for country king and queen
Over the mountains sea and under the sky
They said to you and the others don't ask why
Oh daddy daddy why did you go
Or listen to them for now you know
If you can look down too late you can see
That nothing has altered and inevitably
Lives are not sacred for above vultures still fly
Oh daddy daddy why oh why did you have to die
On the battlefields over sixty years ago
They didn't care for your lives for they couldn't know
That twenty one years after when we'd forgotten it all
Another war was declared too many people and a pall
Of horror again fell over those left behind
Not only did they take the survivors but tried to find
Reasons to justify killing of humanity
Daddy you remember they said we'd all be free
We all believed them for we still didn't see
How we were duped just like now as they said
Fight for your rulers as blood runs red
Oh daddy daddy you never tucked us up in bed
We grew up to believe all we heard and read
As the rich and famous turned their heads away
Pushing us under the carpet as they do today
Saying fight fight for sovereignty and queen
Daddy you didn't have time to dream
You had no power like us to refuse those kings
As still they squabble over the silliest things
And our families are torn again from our sides to fight
They tell us we're wrong and they are right
But now we see our eyes are open and we'll make the time for you

By banning nuclear wars and poverty to make dreams come true
And we won't fight and we won't kill
We'll banish slavery and we will show
That daddy tho' we didn't know you so long ago
No one will die with a sword or gun in their hand
But will preach and practise peace and love in every land

Dancing pool

As I sat gazing in the pool
The children danced by, going to school
Mary, Jane and Robert too
And the doves began to bill and coo
I listened in a dreamy lazy
Way to the twitter of the birds in the hazy
Blue and the thought crossed my mind
That maybe our ancestors sat hoping to find
Some peace and some tranquillity
Maybe mingled with humility
And wondering if perhaps they too
Tried to make impossible dreams come true
And frustrated hopes of a future peace
To enable humanity to take a new lease
Of life with its beauty and its sorrow
Transcending the unknown riches of tomorrow

Do you know

Do you know what it's like to die at the stroke of a pen
Mightier than the sword wiping out a billion boys and men
Do you know what it's like to look at the sky
And hear the screams as poor 'humans' die
Hide under the ground and know those on high
Are planning a Holocaust as they fly
Do you know what was done
As you lose all your loved ones in two wars not one
And hear thru that horror that 'we' have won
Do you know that it takes two
Two to start it and two to end it too
The futility of it all and there's nothing you can do
Yet they spend millions putting men on the moon
And 'peace' costs nothing they'll learn one day soon

26.5.1991

Down the Mall

We sit down and shiver
Cry enough tears to fill a river
No I won't turn on the telly
On that day not on your nelly
When they all troop down the Mall
Shake hands with their colonel good old pal
It doesn't bring back my dad
Or the other members who suffered as the world went mad
For the sake of a crown and the Commonwealth
They dispensed with all the humanities even their health
No I won't look at them for I know yes ma'am
That they don't care a tuppenny halfpenny damn
You don't know you're born as you bow down
To those ministers and to the Crown
In the First World War which they said
Was a war to end wars and when I got his medals read
That inscription but they never told
What they did to those innocents who died in the cold
Just like we're doing for queen and country today
Quarrel over poppies we can't afford anyway

6.11.1986

Dreams

I sit in my chair and dream, and dream
Till the dawn comes peeping thro', and the gleam
Of the sun appears in the east
And my eyes can then feast
On the beauty as my thousand tears
Disappear and I wonder if all one hears
About the wars and the strife
Are true and if so, why is this life
So hopeless for so many, and not the few
As I wish so much that a new
Wonder of the world would appear
To make us realise how terrible is fear
So unfold your hearts and give all your love
To the millions who like the white dove
Need peace and hope in their short span of life
To stop all those quarrels, that are rife
So give us the strength to stand up and fight
With all of our courage and all of our might
But alas I know these are only dreams
For we lack the courage of our convictions, it seems

9.8.1973

Drifting and falling

The cars go rushing, rushing by
And the leaves just sigh and sigh
Rustling softly in the breeze
As they drift gently from the trees
The sun shines, how beautiful it is
As the weeping willow bows down for a kiss
The children laugh and play and sing
They are so happy that even a king
Could not wish for any more
Were he to fly to the farthest shore
For like the links of a chain
They merge together like summer rain
My heart floats over land and sea
And how happy I will be
As I pass by, and the world
Goes along with flags unfurled
I hear the birds calling, calling
And the leaves drifting and falling
As the cars go rushing, rushing by
I just sigh and sigh and sigh

Meridan, Conneticut, USA, 30.12.1976

Engineered by the 'Top Crew'

I can't believe I'm still alive
As I hear someone sing 'I will survive'
I think of the years when I was young
And millions like me who have done
All the chores and manned the phones
For the ones who have so many homes
I remember when I was only three
And now I know no one wanted orphans like me
They hushed up what they had done to the ones
Who stood up and faced all those guns
And when they had finished with them and they'd become
Useless to the system then it was called war number one
And would you believe they put our mothers away
Shut them up, why did they have to pay
And even then, just like now, I say
Millions were left to cope just like today
Never had a decent home or a family and now
It's useless to cry for still I won't kowtow
As I watch our babes in our land that they say
Has freedom and peace and plenty all the way
Then wake up and step over the vermin on the floor
Identifiable so they say and bills at the door
Hounded and harassed beyond belief it's true
Wonder why we praise monarchs and revenue
After seventy five years up pop our men
Kind-hearted ol' soldiers who also fought for them
As the truth creeps in and no one knows when
If we will survive or even be alive
Tomorrow will be here, oh how can I describe
The chasm and the precipice of war
And once again it's all blamed on the poor
The scapegoats who've starved and still do
With empty cupboards we hear how wonderful are the few

Everyone is beautiful

On the playing fields of Eton, I saw
The same kind of children as before
Parents who sit and clap their hands
Then raise a pen to destroy all those lands
And then I heard someone say
Aren't they beautiful our sons and they
Will join the ranks of the officers who
Will train all the others, not in 'who's who'
And then I really had to speak out
With a great despairing shout
Every child is beautiful, what are you talking about
Even if they're not pampered, or sent to a school
Where everything's paid for, and even a fool
Can obtain a degree if they have a name
And don't have to join the survival game

1.12.1985

Fate at my window

Fate tapped on my window one morning at five
Saying hey there wake up is anyone alive
I opened my eyes from a long nights sleep
Full of dreams with meanings so deep
As I opened the door she took my hand
And I flew with her across the land
The things I saw nearly broke my heart
For from the Dark Ages we're so loath to part
The old and young were not very well
And all had very sad tales to tell
With tormented minds by bills so the few
Could reach the top of the quality queue
I said rather crossly oh leave me alone
Let go of my hand for I want to go home
For I don't want to see any more
I want to close my eyes and shut the door
What I ask, oh what are they suffering for
Fate said to me now you see they can't take any more
So don't give up stay and see
What happens in a world where so few hold the key
And help me to find a permanent cure
For the problems of the people that's for sure
And she smiled at me with her eyes
Saying put back the sun in their skies
And took me gently by the hand
That's when I joined that caring band
Of those who are trying to win
The battles of poverty and of sin
And ever since that day began long ago
When fate took my hand and said let's go
And taps on my window each morning at five
Saying hey there wake up is anyone alive

Taking me gently by the hand
To fly and fly all over the land
Helping each other to love not hate
With that wonderful band who don't sit and wait
But get up get out and find what they can do
To make all of humanity's dreams come true
And wait each morning for that tap at five
A voice saying wake up is anyone alive

Finery and lace

I wash my hands and wash my face
Change into my finery and lace
Clean hands and face are such a sham
For I am only what I am
Put me among the right or the left
And I will surely become bereft
Of senses and humanity I guess
And left to clean up all the mess
At times I'm really quite struck dumb
As like an automaton I've become
Still I think of the human race
Wash my hands and wash my face
In the garden I feel the thorn of a rose
And say something not strictly prose
The dog next door jumps over the fence
I mutter something not much sense
Go away there's a good lad
Talking to myself must be mad
I come in from the garden then once again
Wash my hands and face thoughts still remain
The time passes by and flies into hours
I look at all the trees and flowers
And wonder where my energy's gone
Or how to cope and to go on
For I have no finery and lace
I'm just a member the human race

First they took our hearts, now they've come for the other parts

Why do they blame everything on the poor
And why do they say stick to the law
Why is it that when they find a huge cache
Of drugs or anything anywhere they have a bash
Pretend to look for those wicked things
As they say we'll find them but still it brings
Revenue into the coffers of the Crown
Hang them high or put them down
They confiscate them and I wonder where they go
Up pops a public school minister saying it's the poor you know
Drink and cigarettes are a curse
But they don't stop them for the revenue purse
Make laws to keep shops open day and night
Sell off the products who cares what's right
Blame them for everything as they dance
Hand out invites to stars and presidents for a glance
At silk clad legs or a tailored suit enclosed
In minds with nothing as they exposed
Every facet of misery handed out to man
That is the common ordinary human clan

10.11.1985

Flying by

My thoughts can go to sunny Spain
Or back to days of Abel and Cain
Over the mountains or the plain
To the moon or back again
Or even the jungle and spaces wide
On a camel or donkey ride
Perhaps to Russia or the USA
And I do not have to pay
For I only sit in my chair
To ride in a horse drawn carriage and pair
And all I do is close my eyes
To be transported to the skies
Then to sleep and in my dreams
I laugh and ride on moonbeams
Oh what nonsense I hear you say
But my thoughts are here every day
They give me comfort when I worry
Even if I have to hurry
When the weather is wet or fine
I can go back any old time
And my thoughts go over land and sea
Hoping someone will even listen to me
As my thoughts go flying by
With an almost inaudible sigh

9.3.1965

For a Shilling a day

They marched away for a shilling a day
But they never came back for their pay
No one knew, not even now
What happened to them anyhow
They've told us now that they cannot trace
All the records, strange they disappeared from the human race
And even now no one knows where
Though the poppy fields are still there
Every nationality under the sun
Lost millions, poor fathers and their son
And I wonder what happened to their mothers
We speculate about all the others
They went to France and all over
Left those white cliffs of Dover
And the families then lost all hope
Perhaps one day they'll dispense with the soft soap
Get their priorities right those same ones
Who took those youngsters, gave them guns
Promised them when they came back
They would be alright Jack
All with their shilling, shilling a day
They were told that their pay
Would be there and they believed
Didn't know they were to be deceived
Put equality and peace back a thousand years
In return, gave back slavery and tears
Horror and worse poverty and the poor
All for that shilling a day they took away before
And those who came back are still around today
No homes everything the same as yesterday
Nothing's changed just the value of a shilling a day

6.11.1976

Funny, if, as you say, we're in the EEC, why don't we get the same pay?

I'd like to ask a question please
Dear Maggie, although I sit here and freeze
If we're in the common market, as you say
Why madam, do we not get the equivalent pay?

Funny kind of people

Funny kind of people training dogs to kill
And when they do they say shoot them and still
Funny kind of people they train men to die
And when they're dead praise them to the sky
Funny kind of people make a human embryo
Forget all the ones who're here and can't grow
Funny kind of people fly all over signing pacts
Come home to their lands hiding vital facts
Funny kind of people make lords and peers
Give them more luxury while millions cry tears
Funny kind of people starting all those fights
As so many die to protect human rights
Funny kind of people you may not agree
Put us in prison for not paying the TV licence fee

31.12.1984

Happiness

As I write the following word
About the pen being mightier than the sword
I wonder if millions had the same idea
If the world was cleansed of all its fear
Oh how happy we all would be
If that was so and we could see
Even if no one remembers my name
That we are pawns in life's great game
Where the stakes are happiness and comeliness
And we try to dispense all the loneliness
By the words that come from the heart
Making selfish desires a thing apart
For the pen is mightier than the sword
If we remember the written word

18.9.1993

Heartache

The tears are streaming down my face
As I hear of disasters and hate of race
And all the while figureheads sit
With hard unconcern trying to fit
Their social lives into a pattern of greed
Unmelted hearts of stone while they feed
And the plans they make constitute a great feat
Among society and the elite
Quite unaware of the meaning of life
Or how to make happiness instead of strife
And we wish for a mighty hand to hover over all
Ready to clamp down on the short and the tall
Circling the world in one big embrace
Trying to unite with humility and grace
While minds collide as time reaches into eternity
Leaving behind wonder and shaken complacency
Yet with one step forward to take over the lead
We could bring lasting peace, we so much need
As violence still waits with deprivation at our gate
The heartache continues while we await our fate

14.10.1965

How can they do these things for goodness sake?

Oh we're so wicked, it's not true
When the lights go out, what do we do
We go to the airport, pick up the drugs
Conveniently put there for the little mugs
Rush back for the dole office to open then
We sign on wicked women, girls, boys and men
Then go to the post office to cash your cheque
A few pounds more or less, what the heck
Moonlight by moonlight, or even daylight too
How we find the energy for all these things to do
Of course that's it, I forgot it was us!
We went out in the night and got on a bus
Didn't pay, come up next week, criminal records, hooray!
Never mind, it's like that for the poor everyday
They pay such a lot for us and do you know
We're all kidnappers, rogues and thieves and go
Backwards and forwards, and then under
Hear about disasters and listen to the thunder
If we can buy a telly, then we can see
Talk about those who are dead, or might as well be
Or about those who crumble and can't cope
Absolutely without, no single payment or hope
Then listen to the unjust laws our rulers make
How can they do all these things, for goodness sake

I don't remember if I cried, when my Daddy and Mummy died

I don't remember if I cried
When my poor daddy died
I don't remember if I cried
When my mummy was locked up inside
I don't remember if I cried
When I heard what my rulers tried to hide
I don't remember what they said
As our families were left for dead
I don't remember for I was three
What they did in the wars to billions like me
I don't remember what I thought
When at sixty I heard how they fought
I don't remember what was done
Or how those wars were ever won
All I know is now it's true
I don't remember and don't want to
How billions of men were marched away
I don't remember for it was long ago yesterday
And later on we little knew
We'd have to fight in war number two
I don't remember for now I'm old
We ol' patriots sit in the cold
I don't remember what we've done as we're told
It's all hushed up we've all been sold
I don't remember how or why
Millions sit and starve and die
I don't remember but know tomorrow will come
And realize our rulers are blind deaf and dumb

I hate Sundays

I hate Sundays in Camden Town
All those so called yuppies buying a new gown
Silver, antiques or something to please
Paying through the nose for coffee and teas
Whilst all around, homelessness and people freeze

I look at you

I look at you and I think
That my love is like a drink
That I take and have no power
To stop from growing like a flower
The happiness you bring to me
Makes me think of birds so free
And as I sit alone and blue
All I do is think of you
To make my heart come alive
And strong enough to take a dive
Into the blue of heavens above
And my heart is filled with love
That floats away upon a star
I feel I want to shout hurrah
As I sit and think and dream
And I say and really mean
That you'll be happy as day is done
Until the earth meets the sun
To merge together and bring lasting peace
Then all of the wars will cease
And no longer will we sit and dream
For the world will again be seen
In all its glory for all to see
As I look at you I know it will be
The sun will shine

I say hello, then sit down and cry

I have so many friends Madame they wouldn't suit you
All the down-and-outs alcoholics and tramps too
Poor derelict lonely and all those who sin
Against capitalism and don't know what to do and are in
The position of not knowing where to turn
Oh yes they're all the ones you spurn
I can't go to sleep at night for I know
What it is to be like that and to go
To my peers and my government and say
Please can you give me bread today
And they answer back get up and work
Get your fingers out and don't you shirk
Get on your bikes go down the mines
And the reward will be to blot out the sun that shines
While they eat and make merry like they always do and what's more
Have always done and the simple remedy is war
In the courts and in the home I know
If we the lower classes don't pay for everything we'll go
To a hell on earth a prison where all the bars
Blot out faces and moon sun and stars
While the judges and all the ones run away with the gold
They say keeps them warm but they too will get old
And no manner of wealth will save them from their soul
As it happens to all no matter what the role
And my friends are the down-and-outs for whom I smile
If I have a few shillings then I can help them over a stile
And I'm happy for there's isn't anything that I want
I have everything my family grandchildren and don't pray at the font
For I'm nothing and nobody just a clown
To my country like us all as they pull the skies down
In an effort to take more than they can consume or sell
Their souls to the devil such greed as well

And I go to bed thinking how lucky I am at night
Worrying and wondering are they alright
All those lovely people who've said hello and I've replied
Hello and bless you and then sat down and cried

I walk around and I see

I walk around and I see
So many poor it worries me
I say hello and don't know what to do
For I know they have nowhere to go too
Most of them try so hard
Can't win for as they mark their card
Dole and no homes even no bread
And many haven't got a bed
The roof and sky is open house
No one worries and our rulers grouse
Keep on about how we bring in drugs
Hurt us imprison us we are mugs
They say we fiddle and don't wait
For Rome to burn I wonder why they hate
Wonder what's the difference between them
And us except when it comes to mayhem
I say hello and I say hi
And there's nothing I can do only sit and cry
I know what it's like to wander around
Nowhere to go only work and sleep on the ground
They give so much to so few while the many
Haven't even got a single penny
Blame them for everything put them away
Can't see how we can get money anyway
And I go to bed at night
Wondering are they alright
All those poor poor people then out goes the light

I will give you the most wonderful dream

I will give you the most wonderful dream
That the world has ever seen
Gold and silver cannot buy
I'll make you laugh and never cry
And in that dream you'll be king
Dancing around in a fairy ring
And all the while I'll be near
Watching so you'll never know fear
There'll be no more wars and no more fights
No more wrongs only rights
And greed will never show its face
For good will always win the race
When I give you that wonderful dream
That the world has ever seen

I wonder

I wonder what he thought as he
Went to war across the sea
Leaving wife and children so gay
As he went so far away
I wonder if he knew he'd never come back
Along with Peter John and Jack
As I look at hands raised against the poor
They shout and shout and ask for more
Those wives and children who were so gay
Now so old and becoming grey
I wonder who cared for those poor young things
For whom the bell tolled and rings and rings
As I watch the queen in her finery so fay
At the cenotaph on armistice day
I wonder and wonder as she passes by
Oh give to the living I cry and cry
On the sixtieth anniversary of the soldiers who died
I think of the tears I have cried and cried

10.11.1974

I wonder how they came to be there

I like to think of the mountains up there
Sun moon and stars put there to share
The sea and sky the birds and trees
Flowers sunshine and the bees
Oh I wonder how they came to be there
Those blossoms and scenery so very fair
I look at the sea and think of the deep
Then I lay me down to sleep
And the moon shines up in the sky
Thru' my window he winks his eye
All the stars look down on me
As if they are in sympathy
And I think of people everywhere
Then wonder if they too can share
Beauty on earth and in the skies above
For perhaps they have no time for love
Are too busy fighting to hear the call
Of the babes in summer and the fall
And I reach out my hand to touch a star
Passing by so very far
As the time just flies and flies
And I look at the mountains and the skies
As I wonder how they came to be there
Mountains streams sun moon stars and air
Birds trees flowers and people so fair

19.6.1969

I won't cry, no I won't cry

I won't cry no I won't cry
If those angels in the sky
Pass me by no I won't cry
But if those angels with their dirty faces
Pass me by with their airs and graces
Then I'll cry oh how I'll cry
For I'm old and I've seen so many die
Soldiers sailors and airmen too
And still the ones in who's who
Who take the toys and food and homes
Just take from everyone pick the bones
And you know that my heart
Will stop beating and a part
Of my mind will once again cry
If those angels down here pass me by

I won't hang upside down on the palings

I Won't Hang Upside Down On The Palings
Nor will I chain myself to the railings
Tho' if I thought it would do any good
Perhaps I most probably would
But there's one thing I'd do
And that's perfectly true
Is to stand up for the right
To make the world fit and bright
For all by my pen to spread the word
Of peace and plenty down with the sword
Then no one will need to fight any wars
There'll be no quarrels and no cause
For anyone to be unhappy or sad
If the fruits of the earth are shared be no bad
For there's so much and no justification is there
For hunger and poverty any place anywhere
And no one will hang upside down on the palings
Or even chain ourselves to the railings
For freedom will mean what it says
And bring peace on earth for the rest of our days

21.9.1985

I'll write you a song

I'll write you a song about a bird
The like of which you've never heard
And how to reach up to the moon
Without even a silver spoon
I'll write you a song about the stars
Beautiful music played on guitars
Then about those queens and kings
Puppy dogs tails and puppets on strings
The sunrise there all bathed in gold
The misery of the sick young and old
I'll write you a song about the poor
And the Oliver Twist's who ask for more
A song of children as they play
So gaily into another day
Oh I can write about a million things
Gold and silver and diamond rings
And that song could go on forever
If I thought that I could sever
All those ties the human race
Has to cope with and to face
The greed the poverty and the hate
I'll write you a song that will not date
As I go through all the years
To rise triumphant from the tears
I'll write you a song on how to share
The resources and the earth everywhere
On the values that cannot be bought
And for which billions have fought

28.12.1980 - 13.9.1993

I'll stand by you

I'll stand by you thro' thick and thin
Even if you lose or win
You took my heart when you were small
And I watched with pride as you grew so tall
If friends go I'll still stand by you
I'll stand by you and help you too
Thro' all your life in spite of all
I'll stand by you even if you fall
My hand will hold you to my heart
No matter what we'll never part
I love you so I can't let you go
And hope that you will never know
How my heart dies when you go away
Still I'll stand by you forever and a day
Yes stand by you so staunch and true
And always be close to you
Then I know we'll never part
You'll stay forever in my heart

In letters of red, gold and blue

Engraved upon my heart is I love you
In colours red, gold and blue
And if my heart should ever break
A flashing kaleidoscope it would make
I look at you and think that's why
The sun shines so brightly in the sky
And even when the rain comes down
The rainbow never wears a frown
For engraved upon my heart so true
Are the words that I love you
And when I'm cold and when I'm blue
Into my heart comes the echo of you
That makes me begin to live again
You heal the wounds that cause the pain
Written in letters of red, gold and blue
Indelibly printed, the words 'I love you'

9.8.1971

Is it a nightmare or a dream - Oh mum remember me (1939-45)

I sit and wonder is it a nightmare or a dream
And listen to the loonies who all scream
About Russia, Iraq and all those bods who they say
Must get rid of nuclear weapons today
I look with horror on the faces of rulers who fly away
What will tomorrow bring anyway
If there is one and they survive the horror as they pray
For Christmas to come as they gobble up the universe and eat
And look with satisfaction on that feat
They created and now find they can't compete
They're such idiots for they can't see what they've done
And that they're exploiting our poor son
And that wars are never never won
Now who remembers 'cept ol' soldiers, sailors and too
Airmen who went up and down, marched and flew
And those fools who now sit and debate
About all those countries we should hate
Sell them weapons of the highest category as we wait
Sit down and dream and hear about poor Kuwait
Our leaders love war so much and keep on too
About inflation and the economy as billions who
Still, I repeat, hear the cries of those poor things going down
They were black, white and brown
And wonder why they say there's no money in the kitty
It's the same ol' song that ol' ditty
And still there are millions of OAPs
From the First War suffering so that monarch and peers
Can sit down and say vote for us ol' dear
And too late we realise it's crystal clear
What we've passed on to our wonderful children is nothing but fear
And we still hear cries of the poor things going down in the sea
Saying I love you mum, remember me

Just like that

Another bill falls on the mat
I feel like screaming just like that
They want the rent heat and light
I'm always wrong, never right
I'm going down and down again
And now I can really feel the strain
I look at the cars food and wealth
Wonder why they evade folk like myself
Two arms and legs and presumably a brain
Can feel sadness happiness and pain
Still I Just fight and fight and fight
Stick up for others while Jack's alright
But I never never get anywhere
And if anything's going I'm never there
Like Mother Hubbard my cupboard's bare
Get on a bus or train can't pay the fare
To visit the country is a lovely dream
And if I feel much worse I'm going to scream
If another bill falls on the mat
I'll just scream and scream just like that
And if anyone says I'm British mate
So have a stiff upper lip for you're the bait
You've never had it so good I'll scream again
For being British it seems, will send you insane

30.5.1979

Just shut up

Short memories we have all the time
How many have we killed and how much crime
Hiroshima Vietnam the Aborigines French German Poles
English Irish Scots Welsh American Indians and other souls
Dads and mums uncles aunts of every race
Put them away in some dark dank place
They don't tell anyone what they've done
Hope they forget what they did with a gun
Feather their nests as the world passes by
Oh yes when someone famous dies they cry
But they cover up what they're doing with summits and say hi
Yes we will, no we won't ,as millions die
Eternally talking about Chernobyl dust and the others who will
Laugh all the way to Wall Street and banks as they kill

15.9.1986

Just wake up, you can't win

Every day you can guarantee
All they talk about is ordinary you and me
About how wicked we are, you can bet
And how to catch that wicked set
Then out will come the flying squad
No longer will we have PC Plod
Nor will we rely on good old god
But I fear it'll be just the same
Old technology under a different name
They can't even visualise that the old game
Of prevention if applied would be better than the cure
No time for equality or peace as they lure
All those innocents into that terrible trap
Of we want this and that get out the map
Sit and tell you what they want and how to pay
Snooker, football and horses every single day
Making revenue so that the few
Can profit out of me and you
And we prepare their bunkers as they say
All they want is taxes and pay pay pay
For there's not a single little thing not even a pin
We can get if we don't contribute and fall in
Be like automatons, fight and kill when they say
It doesn't matter what you do they'll get you anyway
So stand up and shout hip hip hooray
Nothing's changed there's no tomorrow there's only today

Kings and castles

Once upon a time when I was small
I dreamed I visited a huge marble hall
Millions of people were standing around
Talking and laughing and making so much sound
And at the far gate there stood a man so grand
Looking at them with a pen in his hand
As they filed towards him in that long queue
I heard him say to each one who are you
What have you done in the world down below
They all said we've ruled every poor so-and-so
And made them slaves and made them go
To their graves with the help of a whip and a gun
Made them work hard that's what we've done
Oh come in said that man and they passed thru'
Until my turn came and he said who are you
I'm nothing and no one no public school I fear
Of no consequence and no business here
No palaces money boats planes or gold bars not in who's who
Love little children and all others too
Then I turned to him and said may I ask who you are
When down on earth what did you do
He said it's no business of yours but no matter I will tell
I was a king who ruled that rabble down below oh so well
I beat them and starved them made them work hard too
Building bridges, roads, palaces and growing food so those who
Are up here in heaven can be so grand
And were the influential and revered when they were on land
So they can stand up here with the power to say
Who shall come in and who shall be sent away
And I looked at him and returned to the land
For I don't like their heaven and don't think it's grand
I'd much rather be with those who build bridges and make roads
Than be up here with the ones who make such immoral codes

Lady luck

When I was young I used to dream
Of a cottage and garden cool and green
Where I could take my kids to play
And they could shout and play all day
But now I'm old and dreams have faded
Eccentric and just a little jaded
For lady luck has passed me by
And I wonder oh I wonder why
As I strain my eyes and search behind
For where she's gone I cannot find
I look and look trees and every nook and cranny
Time has passed and now I'm a granny
Those kids have grown and gone away
Now their sons and daughters want to play
In a garden and cottage by the sea
And I wish oh how I wish it could be with me
Oh lady luck come back again
Come back come back and I'll never complain
Then I'll no longer need to dream
Of that cottage and garden so cool and green

14.10.1982

Let's have a lovely war

Let's have a lovely war
We'll show you what the Tories stand for
At the ballot when you put that cross
Then you'll know who's the boss
Oh Argentina here we come
But I forgot we've already done that one
Where can we go for just one more
A lovely lovely lovely war

12.5.1985

Little Cock Robin

The birds of the air the Cock Robin too
We love you so much we really do
The little Red Breast swells with such pride
As he chirps and glances from side to side
To see that no one comes too near
And his little heart throbs with painful fear
Then comes the snow to make us shiver
But Robin Redbreast is all a quiver
With happiness as he flies away
Merrily into the sky to return another day
And all the other birds come back to
Our shores and oh what to do
If they could tell all the tales
Of mountains streams and beautiful dales

Long ago

I passed by a window one day long ago
And saw all the things spread out on show
Over in the corner right out of sight
I saw a kind heart in the half light
Softly I asked how much it was
And was told no sale just because
First of all it was entirely free
No gold could ever buy it for me
Only the kindness and love of mankind
Equality compassion and peace of mind
No power on earth could make it mine
As I walked away I could see it shine
And I vowed one day I'd take it from that shelf
Then put it back within myself
Away from that dusty shop long ago
Where it sat among the things on show
I'd keep it safe from cold and storm
In the style for which it was born
Now if you look in that shop window there
You won't find it anywhere
Because I went back and took it away
And now it's so happy anyway
So here ends my tale of long ago
About a kind heart put out on show

3rd Avenue, New York, 21.12.1977

Love

When you call I will always come
Rushing to your side to become
Your help through thick and through thin
I will climb the mountain and face the din
Of voices raised in anger or disdain
And will always help to bear the pain
Or laugh, if you so desire
And my feet will never tire
Of following you even though you say
You do not want me to stay
Or the obstacles are so high
And will always make me sigh
For my love will never die
As I gaze into the sky
Then close my eyes to sleep and wake
To another day till it's time to take
The last road disappearing round the bend
The one to which there is no end

Memory lane

The most beautiful thing on this earth
Is the smile of a child and their laughter and mirth
The sparking eyes which defy
The gods looking down from the sky
And the happiness that they bring
With songs in their hearts floating on the wing
Of beautiful birds flying high as a kite
Higher and higher up to the light
As I go with you down memory lane
The laughter of children will ever remain

19.9.1993

Millionaires are out of date, it's Billionaires this year

I have friends and relations in high places
And I look with horror on their faces
I see the poor old drunks and tramps too
And I think whatever can I do
Why oh why can they not buy
That kingdom they say is in the sky
I see all of those people old and young
Sitting in four walls, listening to that forked tongue
Of those ministers, as they fly
All over the world, and I cry and cry
As I hear them say with great glee
I'm buying a house or car, we're free
And then I wonder, what's wrong with me
As I don't want those things for you see
There's nowhere I can take them anyway
When as eventually I go away
No one on this earth want's to leave, no way
And I can't see the difference anyway
At that pagan feast that comes around each year
When millions have nothing and once more I hear
Of new year honours of those who do their best, I fear
To cheat and steal those lives in wars
And then tell us all to rush to the stores
You're so lucky and I wonder why
Beauty is only in the beholders eye

Misery

As into the doctors surgery I go
The faces around me have no glow
And no one even deigns to speak
Maybe because they feel too weak
Or they think that we should be
Better off if we're set free
From all the ailments from which we suffer
But there I'm such a silly old duffer
To think the world would be a better place
If folk were friendly with smiles on their face
So out of the surgery I do go
Into the street where the wind doth blow
Seeing all those faces filled with misery
Is to me an inexplicable mystery

24.5.1979

Moonbeams

They brought me flowers and their eyes
Shone like moonbeams from out of the skies
I could not speak for my heart was full
For they were as precious as any jewel
Tho' jaded and dying from little hands
They were held together with grassy strands
My heart was so light as I thought
Of the love that they had brought
Into my life with a kiss
And a room filled with laughter I miss
So much when they go away
I long for them so much to stay
Oh I wish I wish I wish
They would stay for then the bliss
Would last forever and a day
For as they always say
There is no tomorrow
Bringing joy and sorrow
As I gaze at the beautiful skies
And wish I could keep those moonbeams in their eyes

1969

Morning comes

Morning comes and I open my eyes
And look into the beautiful skies
Then I think oh what's the use
As I make some silly excuse
For me thinking all those things
And wondering whatever the future brings
I start on the chores of my day
Sorting out the bills to pay
My daydreams stop and I have to hurry
Old man time never seems to worry
I brush away those hidden fears
As the morning passes and disappears
Then I come home and I sit
Thinking how life just galls a bit
Then a knock comes upon the door
I go back to my dreams once more
And see myself with sword in hand
Fighting dragons so I can stand
To face another morning as it comes
Like the rushing river as it runs
And open my eyes to the light
From the long long silent night

11.1.1973

Mr Nobody

Oh how they stop and how they stare
At Mr nobody all tattered and threadbare
And I see they're sometimes amused
At the poor thing who's so confused
I wonder who cares for all the ones
Who came back without the guns
For all they do is stop and stare
At Mr nobody all tattered and threadbare
The sky's his roof and the ground his bed
Oh where can he lay his weary head
Once or even twice he went to war
Now he wonders what it was all for
Hungry and tired he wends his way
Going nowhere night and day
And I cry and I cry
As he slowly passes by
And see all those who stop and stare
As he slowly goes nowhere
And of those days when he used to fight
When he was young and the sight
Of a flag and king and of queen
And that country that once was seen
As good and kind and would help one day
like millions he finds now it's not anyway
For there's only the open road and no bed
Homes or anything not even bread

11.1.1974

My friend

She stretched out her hand and said my friend
I wonder if she knew how much those words meant
They pierced my heart as did cupid of old
And raised me to the heights like knights so bold
The world of elegance was in her smile
For which I could have walked for many a mile
My clothes did not matter I felt like a queen
Such goodness of heart was there to be seen
As I looked around the world was pure gold
I walked on air how I reached the ground I'm told
Was a miracle as I walked home in a haze
As round and round I went in a daze
Still I can feel that kind hand and can hear
As she called me her friend it rings in my ear
When the world of elegance came to town
Enfolding me in her satin and silken gown

My heart is a bird

When the bombs dropped I was sitting
With my children and my knitting
My heart beat fast like a bird
As I thought about the horrors I had heard
About boys being made to fight
Against what was wrong, or was it right
English and foreigners killing each other
Maybe their sisters or their brother
All nations secretly longing for peace
And wishing the hostilities would cease
Why don't they turn the other cheek
Maybe because they are too weak
Or wish to save the explanations
While giving out exhortations
Don't do this and don't do that
And giving back tit for tat
They never dream of shaking hands
Or singing and cheering with the bands
Wishing all the hate would cease
So that they can live in peace
Kissing each other on the cheek
The strong the mighty and the weak

1984

My heart is lost

My heart is lost, I feel no pain
As I walk bareheaded in the rain
My footsteps falter out of line
And feel as if no longer mine
Thoughts come rushing to my mind
Not always good and not always kind
Forming a pattern only I can weave
Reminding me of the past I cannot leave
Your words come back again and again
As I walk bareheaded in the rain
Walking along I laugh and cry
Thinking of your words as I pass by
But you have gone I know not where
I put out my hand and you're not there
My footsteps falter again and again
For I've lost my heart but feel no pain
I wonder wonder where are you
And that you can be so untrue
As I walk bareheaded in the rain
For I've lost my heart but feel no pain
So if you find my heart please send it to me
Then once again I shall be free
To keep my heart without the pain
And walk bareheaded again in the rain

9.8.1965 - 28.12.1975

My Postman

He brings me letters from my friends
Bills as well welcome or otherwise that depends
I sit and wait for his knock on the door
As I have no bell no not any more
He makes me feel I'm someone again
Even thro' anguish and the pain
I only hope that when he's old and grey
No one will turn around and go away
And will not only give him the tea
They also will bring him all the sympathy
For the good tidings or ill he brings
As he goes like Hercules on feet with wings
Taking me to heaven in a daily race
In my rush to see his cheery face

My three wishes

If I had three wishes I know what I'd do
The first would be to stay with you
Always always to be by your side
And never never never to hide
Up in the skies in a golden cloud
All covered by a misty shroud
The second would be to stay good and true
With kindness and love all my life thro'
And to see the happiness in your eyes
Never to be sad or blue when you rise
Always to see your beauty when I awake
But the third and last wish I would make
Would be to stop all the wars
To seriously think and to pause
Before doing anything to hurt
Or perhaps with fate to flirt
And these three wishes I would have for you
With kindness and love your whole life thro'
As over the world you go and fly
Giving my three wishes to everyone passing by

My World

They'll put me in prison so they said
And only give me water and bread
Water and bread that's what they say
And that's the way they'll make me pay
I've got to mind my P's and Q's
Or they will give me permanent blues
As they recite the dos and don'ts
I tell them of my wills and won'ts
But they only turn a deaf ear
To my cries and they're blind I fear
For when I say what I want to do
They say oh who oh who are you
To want to make the world so fair
For the ones already there
Who have no goods or milk and honey
You even want to give them money
But one day I will have this
In my world of happiness and bliss

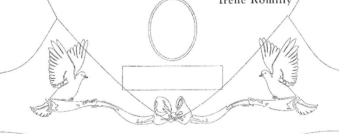

Irene May Romilly
30th May 1915 - 24th August 1994

No flowers, no flowers please when I go
No not for me the ostentatious show
Just have me always in your heart
Although so very far apart
Don't say mean things you will regret
Just think of all the things which can beset
Us all in spite of how we rise or fall
So if you feel sad about it all
Think only of those wonderful times
When you were young and sang your simple rhymes
And you made me so happy and glad
That I alone was all you had
As all I ever want is your love
So wherever I go below or above
Your heart will always be with me
So please, no flowers, just to please me.
Irene Romilly

No place to hide

I saw a shooting star one day
It came from oh so far away
Falling falling so swiftly down
Looking like a diamond crown
I waited in vain for it to reappear
My vision obscured by a tiny tear
Then awoke to reality from my dreams
With the stars veiled in mystery it seems
As I gazed at the beauty all around
With peace serenity and the sound
Pervading the vastness of the sky and sea
And a shooting star coming right out at me
From oh so far across the great divide
For where is there a place to hide
From the stars put there for me and you
To guide us in whatever we do
As over the universe so wide so wide
There's simply no place a shooting star can hide

9.3.1979

North and South

You can send me north and send me south
But you can never put words in my mouth
You can make me cry or even sigh
And even you can pass me by
Perhaps accuse or abuse
Or make any old excuse
To make me angry or to smile
Even join the rank and file
So send me north and send me south
But you can never put words in my mouth
You can come and you can go
Or take me to a picture show
Flatter me or raise my hopes
Or take me to the snow covered slopes
Take me to the Alps or Rome
Even give me a marvellous home
Send me north or send me south
But you can never put words in my mouth
Tho' perhaps you won't agree
Those words will be as clear as can be
And what I say will always be true
The same as my thoughts and what I do

31.5.1970

Not dead yet

No matter how hard they try
Offering cash if you die
Or if you don't you'll still get
Missiles bombs and the Exocet
Unless you all stand up and fight
Against the loonies who take the light
From the stars sun and sky
And place a mote into the human eye
Take the resources from the land and sea
Then wave the flags and say you're free
And no matter how hard they try
No we won't, we won't die
Don't let the monsters take our human race
Can't substitute them for arsenic and old lace
And there's no way, no way you can bet
For as you see, I'm not dead yet

1984

Not in Who's Who

I went to the coroner and I said
Could you please examine me before I'm dead
He looked at me thought I was out of my head
I think he thought I wanted my bumps read
I went to the doctors surgery he wasn't there
And I can assure you that goes on everywhere
But only in the lower estate
Call again tomorrow she said as if I didn't rate
I went to the House of Commons to see my MP
So many cops we know we're not free
What have you got in your bags let's look
Only papers I said I'm writing a book
I came out and went to the Cenotaph so near
An official said what are you doing here
I looked at him filled with fear
Wondered how I'd survived to reach my seventieth year
I went across the road to number ten
Saw nine cops and then
Asked one where the prime minister was and when
She'd be back he was most surly and said
What's it to you I felt like saying drop dead
I walked away to Trafalgar Square
At least the pigeons were free to fly anywhere
Without their permission to be alive
Just then I found it hard to survive
Went back home the gas had been cut off altho'
It's not much use when it's on it won't go
I'm so used to going without heat or light
Continually told it'll be alright
Nothing wrong just too bad for you
Are in the situation of catch twenty two
Take my word for it there are thousands too
In the same situation not it who's who

Now I know

Today I know that the older I grow
The more things I know
I'm wiser but realise it's true
That it's not what you know but who
And money is the be-all and too
The end and I wish I knew
What's in store for the young
As the politicians become more deaf and dumb
On the priorities we're told we've won
As millions come back from wars not one
But two and struggle to feed their children as the who
Sit down and say we're so unhappy for you

16.2.1994

No way no way

Charity begins at home or so they say
You don't have to be good or clever to give away
Or share with another what man has grown
To give out bread instead of a stone
Hail kings or lords or those who have all the wealth
And make for poverty as into minds with stealth
They creep thru' the day and at night
Plan deadly deeds to worsen the plight
Of the ones who have no earthly power
To say yea or nay as lives daily grow sour
For if man steals food it stands to reason
He's practising self-preservation not treason
And all the judges do is make them pay
For in the first place they couldn't so there's no way
They could be punished for again and again
And over and over they condemn it's always the same
As millions are stolen and nothing's said
But if a poor man steals milk or bread
In the past he could even be put in the Tower
Or the powers-that-be cry hang them then reprieve at the eleventh hour
The ones who make so much money then leave
To avoid paying tax then come back to receive
More as they say we'll give it to charity give away
But forget that charity begins at home
And sing about democracy and give a dog a bone
As the purse gets full and they smile
But their eyes are hunting out the shekels as mile by mile
The years go by and nothing alters
The race against time goes on and never falters
And one day our children will look up and say
Oh who were those people who spoke about charity yesterday
For they never helped those in need
All they did was sow that deadly seed

Officer officer

Officer officer arrest me please
Hurry up before I freeze
Lock me up in a nice clean cell
Radio colour TV there are meals as well
Soap towels shampoo and clean clothes
Oh! What luxury heaven knows
Can't escape no passport anyway
Families massacred long ago yesterday
Simpletons then now we are wise
Can see the inner evil of their eyes
Laugh as the old and the young
Die of deprivation one by one
So officer officer arrest me please
For now she's won we'll all freeze
No G.L.C no one at all
While ministers and monarchy go to the ball

27.3.1986

Oh, 'Daddy Daddy' (06.11.1918, *Daddy you were 23* and I was only 3*)

Daddy daddy didn't have time to dream, took you to fight for King country and Queen,
Over the mountains and under the sky, oh daddy had no chance to ask why,
Daddy daddy didn't have to go and listen to them for now we know
Twenty one years they've forgotten it all, daddy did you have to fall

Things can change, things will change, things are changing

On the battle fields sixty years ago they couldn't care they couldn't know,
That over our lives the vultures still fly, daddy did you have to die
Yet another war, thousands will fall, how could they forget it all
The horror of those left behind, the survivors they tried to find
Reasons to justify the killing of humanity, don't you remember they said we'd be free

Things can change, things will change, things are changing

Daddy daddy never tucked us up in bed, grew up to believe all we heard and read
Fight fight fight for sovereignty and Queen, I know it's all a dream
We won't fight, we won't kill, we refuse to act out their will
We won't die with a gun in our hand, but practice and preach love in every land

Things can change, things will change, things are changing, NOW!

Lyrics by Irene Romilly 11.11.1991

* *Frederick William Romilly was actually 29 when he died in Etaples, France, 6th November 1918, when Irene wrote this poem she mistakenly thought he was 23. Oh Daddy Daddy, Lyrics Irene Romilly 1991, song created and performed by Mimi, © 2014, available from mimi-uk.com*

Oh my daughters oh my sons

Oh my daughters oh my sons
Brothers and sisters put down those guns
Don't go to war and don't you fight
Only with words to promote right
Oh my daughters oh my sons there's so very very much
On this earth for us all you don't need that Midas touch
So give us bread instead of a stone
Look after the living why should they atone
Don't fight for the ones who take all the time
And find pleasure in promoting envy and crime
Oh my daughters, sisters and mums
Brothers, uncles, fathers and sons

23.4.1990

Our World is here and so are we

I had a dream that's going to come true
To involve all those who need a friend or two
I've sat and thought of a plan
To help all those sons of man
Food in plenty not only on one or two days
To erase all those tears and not just a phase
I want to look on the beautiful face
Of man and woman all over the place
The demon drink is banned for all time
For revenue or gold it will be a crime
And I won't hear of a bomb or a gun
Or wars or battles lost or won
For no one can win or even lose
In a scientific game if they abuse
The laws of gravity and of space
By eliminating the whole human race
'Cause there's peace and plenty for everyone
And my dream will come true without a gun
Even tho' our rulers roam the world and say
We won't give up our sovereignty or go away
For it's only the ones who have no power
Who pay and hear them chant now is the hour
Equality and hope is beyond their grasp
As the flag is raised and with their last gasp
Our soldiers say look after them, look after them
Our families friends and poor mice and men
Don't worry about a new world or where we go
Just make every hour everyday show
Our world is here and so are we with God's grace
And we love our wonderful human race

24.12.1983

Out of sight

You walk on the left or on the right
But never never will you shut out the sight
Of birds and trees or the plain
Or the earth or stop the human brain
You may kick or stamp or scream
Or you can say what you really mean
But never will you shut out the sight
Of human misery or the sad plight
When a stream becomes a flood
And people erupt amid rivers of blood
Fighting the dragons in their mind
Forgetting to be good and kind
Trying to see what's hidden out of sight
Whether you walk on the left or the right

Out of the ordinary

I went to the cupboard and it was bare
And tomorrow I haven't even my fare
So it's a walking tour for me I guess
As I go the rounds oh what a mess
And then as I go home again
After aimlessly walking in the rain
I'm just too sick with wanting to be
Someone out of the ordinary
Instead of being just a pawn in the game
And wishing I had someone again
But it's still that old feeling in my brain
Just like a poor wounded bird
Whose cry for help can never be heard
And I cannot even speak a word I fear
For there's none so deaf as those who will not hear

Pandora's box

You can lock up from a thief they say
But from a liar there is no way
He creeps inside your mind I'm told
Taking away more than all the gold
Insidious words beat thru' your head
As you lie awake thinking of the things they said
Those promises of house and car
Visits to places near and far
Oh don't you know those words can kill
And those lies spoken at will
I do not say I like a thief
But at least his reign is brief
But words we speak are here forever
And even tho' we are not clever
They go with us everywhere
Bring us health wealth and care
So before you speak pause for you're not a fox
Before you open up Pandora's box
Letting those lies float away so high
Far away over mountain sea and sky
For every time you tell those lies
Someone somewhere fades and dies

6.2.1975

Please send me a copy of our Human Rights

Could you send me a copy of our human rights please
I seem to have mislaid it along with the keys
I can't remember it's so long ago
Did we ever get a copy I don't know
It's only ten years since I knew
What happened to our forefathers and joined the queue
For justice and even enough to eat
And since the Tories have been here there's not even heat
Please send me a list of those human rights
Sorry for the mistakes no 50p for the lights
Tea and bread no butter because it's there
Hoarded up in the Common Market I declare
Plenty of brains now it's too late for everywhere
There are markets galore all over the place
Missiles and nuclear to wipe out the human race
And I wonder for I have no photograph
Why I can't even visit the cenotaph
I didn't even look at it on the telly
Don't want to I've got a rumbling belly

11.11.1986

Please take it away

Every night and every day I pray
Take this horror nuclear away
Tho' I don't know or care
How those zones operate anywhere
Tell the ministers and banks put it back
Don't be greedy empty the sack
Don't tell me there's a god up there
I don't want to know and I don't care
So has the great bear always been there
For a million billion years
Watching the laughter tragedy and tears
So I don't care to whom I pray
Or if there ever was a doomsday
All I know is we're here today
And gone tomorrow so they say
And I ask can the gods tell the sky
Some fools are wanting the universe on high
Told to vote for this and that
So a few can carry on tit for tat
Or hold the flags aloft and pray
For the monarchs and make us pay
A flag of red and one of red white and blue
One for the fools like me and you
Tell us how to vote and then say
Endlessly what they want to do today
Go to hounds and hunt the foxes
Then come back and put our young and old in boxes

Rain and storm

I'm keeping those kisses in my heart every day
Those kisses those kisses I tuck them away
And when I'm cold they keep me warm
Safe from the rain and from the storm
For you came from heaven and blue skies
And all I can see are your glorious eyes
When I'm down you raise me so high
I feel those kisses and no longer sigh
And remember the words you say to me
I love you, I love you, so much as you see
I'm trying to make all your dreams come true
For your sweetness is like the summer dew
So I'm tucking those kisses in my heart away
Those kisses, those kisses, I get every day
And when I'm cold they keep me so warm
Safe from the rain and from the storm
Those kisses are with me as I go all over the land
You run away with them in your little hand

19.3.1976

Razzmatazz

I'm puzzled by the news
Of those long held views
That the suffering public hold
All about the knights of old
Princes, princesses, kings and queens
With our nightmares making their dreams
Billions a year from revenue untold
And the Moslem's oil, black gold
The arms race too, we now hear
How much was made every year
Selling to all and sundry, I fear
And now it's all coming out
What a lot of idiots, those with clout
They've let the cat out of the bag
Just a silly old public school rag
Too late to invoke the secrets act
You know the one that hides every fact
Inflation that good old standby too
Deflation and poverty to get rid of you
They raise their eyes to the heavens above
Tell us that it's all god's love
That will protect us as the pope flies in
To tell us all that we sin
In his finery and his lace
And enough rhetoric to kill the human race
Clad in gold and all that jazz
Kissing the ground and all that razzmatazz

Redundancy

It creeps like a thief in the night
This fear that stalks until the waking light
They call it by a new fangled name
Redundancy oh who's to blame
The machines that creep insidiously
Or humanity that religiously
Proclaim that all's well for the Lord
Is in heaven so all must be right with the world
When buildings are erected almost overnight
To stand as achievements of human might
Whilst redundants and others watch with awe
And constantly unwittingly break the law
In order to try and fight what they fancy
Is caused by uselessness and redundancy

Ring around my heart

Kindness never hurts nor does it sting
For it forms a lasting ring
Around my heart that ties a knot
Never to be untied no matter what
We do and it takes away all cares
As we go on thro' the years
But pierce the ring around my heart
Then I'd feel I'm in a world apart
For if the ring should ever break
It would leave a long dull ache
So let me keep that golden ring
I'll rise to heights unknown and sing
As the ring around my heart just glows
Brightly as the older it grows
And even if you haven't a thing
You can still have that golden ring

Roses, roses round the door

I see the roses round the door
Oh how I wish that I had more
And tho' I know it's all a dream
I can even see a stream
Where I can sit as roses bloom
And as I sit in my lonely room
I see a cottage as I stare
A horse carriage pumpkin and bear
A groom as I sit in beautiful clothes
Honeysuckle and the scent of a rose
And as my eyes get used to the light
Magical colours come into sight
The sun's so hot and the breeze so cool
I can see a garden and a pool
And my children oh so small
I look again and they're oh so tall
Then I awake and no one's there
No horse groom cottage pumpkin or bear
Honeysuckle or even roses round the door
It's all the same as it was before
The sun's so hot and the breeze so cool
There's no garden and no pool
No honeysuckle or roses round that cottage door
It's all just the same as it was before
But those children have gone away
And they didn't have time to play
The pattern is repeated for I've never seen
Or had a cottage with roses for it's all a dream

Safe Inside

I'll shut the door and go inside
And then I'll find some place to hide
Away from all those trivial things
And the sorrow that life brings
Hiding my thoughts as they come and go
They are like the strings of a bow
Out of tune, and sometimes inane
As sanity prevails they still remain
Reminding me of broken dreams
And of life and all it means
So I'll go inside and shut the door
Safe from all even the law
And when the summer comes again
With its beauty, the sun and the rain
I'll come out and breathe and sigh
Dancing along as I laugh and cry
My eyes will see as if born again and new
I'll see the trees and feel the dew
As another year passes by I will live again
With mind refreshed and my brain
No longer tired, singing with happiness and bliss
For I have lived, just lived for this

Seventy thousand troops marched up and down

Seventy thousand troops are going to be deployed
Costing millions and I suppose all those unemployed
And I really wonder are they quite sane
For they want more wars, oh no not again
They said before we fight for peace and no more
Will we have another war and they swore
Never never and each year all dressed up they cry
Crocodile tears for all our boys who die
Fight and quarrel who shall put a wreath on the Cenotaph
Then disperse into a Rolls Royce where they're able to have a laugh
Eat and eat and eat and take and take
Sit and talk about what they can make
Go all over making laws and plans
Drink the elixir of life and make bans
Don't do this and don't do that
Natter natter natter playing tit for tat
Send their families to the best schools
Don't worry about the others they're all fools
For they know if they pull the strings we all dance
As we've always done all over Europe and France
Everywhere they can raise a finger and we'll all be gone
There's nothing we can do for they always con
The masses as they did in the days of old
When all those kings and dukes were so bold
Marched their thousand troops up and down
Over the mountains and the plains for a crown
They marched them up and then marched them down again
Now they're doing it once more it's still the same
So they can boast good old Britain fly the flag
Dole and medals bronze silver gold for a tag
Round the necks of all those poor young boys
So they can use those ultra expensive toys
Exocets and nuclear taking the place of guns
Changing the face of the earth with our expendable human sons

11.09.1984

Shares, shares, shares, but not ours, theirs

Empty vessels make the most sound
Do they suggest the simpler round
Or maybe say visit Barrow-in-Furness for our health
Or the other hospitals they say were built from our wealth
Their standard of living we know is high
Perhaps they'd like to sit and cry
Whenever all the lights goes out
And all those capitalists they do shout
Bring back hanging and a deterrent
They always talk rubbish, it's inherent
How long does it take to blow millions away
A few seconds you couldn't even pray
No time to keep complaining about the others
It will affect them all, sisters, brothers, fathers and mothers
And when that wicked regime was in power, you know
I had enough to eat a bath, heat and lights didn't go
But of course it's that old seven-year itch
And there was no trouble on the football pitch
And they will say oh, no, no, no
That's not true they forgot you know
But we have very long memories and remember too late
Every day, every year, from that date
When we were abandoned by our rulers to fate
And all they can cite is what others do
And I notice that they are all in who's who
But not my type I'm afraid no way
For I can see into the mentality that will blow us away
But first of all they must have the shares
And make sure the youngsters can't get theirs

10.10.1986

Spinning around

That kiss upon my cheek still lingers
With the touch of those little fingers
Remaining while the sound of feet
Rush to meet with open arms to greet
Me at the door spinning me round and round
Until my head starts to pound
But I will never never never never
Remove that kiss even if I live forever
So remember when you get that kiss
The gold of her hair and the joy in his eyes
Which brings to mind the sunshine and skies
As I lay down to sleep and awake to a new day
While the sun shines to help me on my way
With love in my heart that's to be found
As my head spins round and round and round

1980

Stand up sister, stand up brother, stand up for each other

Stand up sister, stand up brother
Just stand together, stick up for each other
One meal, one house and car is enough for all
There's plenty for everyone, you don't need a haul
Stand up for your neighbour and everyone
Don't listen when they tell you to pick up a gun
Life is the most precious thing
Much more important than anything
If we don't stand together, we'll be no more
And become victims of those enemies of the poor
Who by all human rights, should not be there
For there's so much for everyone, everywhere
No one will need a bunker to get away
If only they were satisfied to live day by day
Having enough is far better than a feast
For no one should go without or make do with the least
And to be the richest person is obscene, it can't be
With legs, hands, ears and eyes, you can see
Is enough with that brain for the average you and me
And the added value of having the other guy around
Is to dig up and see the sky and what's in the ground
We can't take it with us, wherever we go up or down
Whether you're that pauper or someone with a crown
So stick together - we're wonderful whether black, white or brown

Still don't know what happened in Etaples, France now it's 1991

Started out with nothing left severely alone
Don't know why since then I've had to atone
Had no dad or even a brother
Uncle aunt cousin or mother
I heard later there were sisters four
Would you believe there was a law
That covered up all the facts of the First War
Yes it's strange but true
And there's no one to answer to
The ones who plundered and murdered too
Are still here or their minions and we never knew
What was done and don't know now
Tho' it's very hard to conceive how
It's possible as we're told they are heroes anyhow
Old soldiers still here told me what transpired and what they heard
In the camp named Etaples in France where massacres occurred
Old soldiers they said never 'died' but only faded away
And now the defence ministry don't know what to do anyway
For the survivors are asking questions today
To which they can't give an answer, for they
Could be prosecuted like all the others and have to pay
Like those all over the world who've done the same
But not nearly as bad as our constant war game
That was repeated so many times and under a different name
For the ones responsible have no shame
Interfere in their anxiety to pass the blame
On to everyone and now their victims a billion or more
Sit and wonder and die of poverty in the majesty of that criminal secrets act of law

1.1.1991

Such a strange phenomenon

Such a strange phenomena they set
The less you do the more you get
And the less you have it's true
Rules your fate whatever you do
And all you get is pie in the sky
Broken promises up on high
March to war is the cry
If you have they just say
Think of tomorrow not today
Then they take your minds away
Write or phone us they say
Passports holidays pay pay pay
Millionaires pop up and say
We live to fight another day
For us no dollars and not even pounds
Just get up and do the rounds
Brothers you cant's spare a dime
For you've made that pantomime
Bring out the pawns and play the game
For it will always be the same
The less you do the more you get
It's such a strange phenomenon they set

17.8.1985

Take me, oh take me

Take me oh take me she screamed at the pitiless skies
Her hair turned white I can still hear her cries
Such tragedy in those years of a second world war
Inhuman and useless just like the one before
All for nothing as the peace we craved so long
Never even materialised and the song
Has been carried farther and farther away
So many poor and hopeless today
My mind is still fresh as that first bomb came
Landing in the road hitting the gas main
No buildings came down but all were trapped and died
I stood surveying the scene with my child and cried
Beside a poor soul so very sad
For she'd gone to get food for sons and dad
Who joined up to fight a world gone mad
The siren sounded and caught us unawares
The moon shone down on those trapped like hares
We were so innocent waved the flag like sheep
Where were our rulers who left us again to weep
As the horror sunk in I shouted stop and cried
To the heavens above I could have died
I thought about all the others
Made to fight sisters and brothers
Of whatever nationality it's all the same
For it takes two to make a war to our eternal shame
As I look back I know all they think of is fame
Pound dollar and dime and the sun and stars in the skies
I tried to shut out the awful cries
Of those who were trapped under the ground
But all I could hear was that terrible sound
Peace came passed over our heads and passed on
And now I'm old I realise it has always gone

As we fight over nothing anyway
So monarchs and rulers can have their way
Never stop praising war and their crimes
Since the days of ancient times
And I remember that day in September I stood with my son
Then turned and ran from the carnage of what we'd done
Screamed out at the skies peace and plenty is there for everyone

That twenty two carat Sun

There's a golden twenty-two carat sun
Shining up in the heavens having so much fun
As round and round and round it goes
Chasing the wind as it gaily blows
All over the world it rises and shines
It travels the highways and state lines
Shines and fades day by day
Thousands of millions look up as away
It goes a million million million miles
Over fields forests and stiles
The earth and sea cannot escape
They're encircled as by a giant tape
Measuring the waves flowers and trees
Chasing shadows over dales and leas
It never stands still just like old father time
No voice to quote reason and rhyme
And like a clock it's always there
Behind those clouds it hides somewhere
That beautiful gold twenty-two carat sun
Whose face disappears when day is done

30.6.1980

That's all I want

How can I tell you that all I want
Is to love every child not pray at the font
To give them a piece of my heart every day
Peace and plenty every step of the way
Good homes clothes toys and sweets too
Play from morning to night not only for the few
How can I make their dreams come true
Wipe away their tears for that's the clue
To the abolition of wars and hate
Making equality the aim for all as they wait
And watch or whatever they do while the law
Works so hard to destroy them by war
Give them freedom of mind and to all the others
Don't dictate just be kind to fathers sons and mothers
Sisters daughters and brothers and stop taking
Just give for a change instead of making
Poverty misery of body heart mind and scorn
As they push them down from the day they're born
What can I say when those up above look down
With contempt as they speak to everyone and frown
Saying don't show me up as I have a position to maintain
House and comfort the neighbours will complain
And I look and my heart goes bumpety-bump
Sinks into my boots and beats like a pump
How can I tell them all I really want
Is peace and love of my children not to flaunt
Fine clothes painted face or diamond rings
A huge bank account or hobnob with kings
Fill my head with luxuries or sit on a throne
Only want to take everyone as they come and condone
Their shortcomings for we all have those you know
As we go through life and it goes to show

That humanity is good bad weak or even strong
But in the end no one can survive for long
Without the heart and the hands of common man everywhere,
You know it I know it make those who take the lions share
Stop and take stock of the actions that give them power
To destroy and desecrate that human flower

5.12.1983

The 6th November a jinx to me

The stamps have gone up a penny today
Another thing to make the public pay
And Guy Fawkes night is coming near
I think perhaps I won't be here
But maybe I'll wait till the 6th for on that day
My great-great-great-grandfather died, they say
And I didn't even know anyway
Of his existence and how great he was yesterday
Then I found out after sixty years of despair
My father was killed and families vanished into thin air
On that very day I still have the medals I got
In 1976 and that was my lot
And I heard last year, my son died of diabetes in Rio
That was on the 6th November too, a trio
Can't visit the graves of my dear dad or son
To grieve for their lives that had just begun
Too far away, one in South America, one in France
Oh, what can I do? I haven't got a chance

30.10.1986

The bank manager

He comes towards me with a smile and outstretched hand
As I advance and sit down at his command
Waiting with bated breath as his smile fades
As I ask for an overdraft his face turns different shades
He stutters and stammers and at last he says
What collateral have you for in all my born days
I could not advance a penny for you can see
How hopeless the position would be for me
As no security can you supply
So how could you repay if you suddenly die
So creeping out I hide inside my despair for
Oh what a sin it is to be so poor

The blind man

I hear a tapping on the ground
The urgency makes me look around
Then I see a man who's blind
And thoughts come rushing to my mind
What I say is in his brain
Perhaps a void to bear the strain
Of facing another hour or day
In which to work or to pray
Or maybe as he struggles with his Braille
There will be no time to rail
Against the fate bestowed upon him
For although his eyes are dim
He may be a better man within

The bright lights

They talk about human rights
Then go home to their bright lights
Living off the fat of the land
With all facilities to hand
Every time I hear they strike gold or oil
Or strike it rich it makes my blood boil
Then they say tighten your belts
Picts Scots English and Celts
Good old British or are we perhaps
Europeans caught in deadly traps
We must have stocks and shares and wars
For their luxuries to come to their doors
Brave their anger if we criticise
Where our taxes go or want a rise
Raise standards from the ground to the heights
Regardless of class to give all human rights
To us all they can't see we're all the same
Even if we do not have a famous name
We can't expect three meals a day
Or like our ministers fly away
To Japan or any place even Commonwealth Games
In coats of many colours and different names
When there's a shortage of any commodity they cry
Use things like water sparingly or die
I look at them and wonder do they hear
But the answers in the negative I fear
For I know misery and poverty prevails
And they can't see my heart just quails
How can they reconcile the right to be fed
Why should we starve for we don't want to be dead
The world is our oyster and no one has the right
To more than enough or to take the light

Away from the eyes of anyone or stand up and praise a lord
And really don't mean a word they say or accord
Those simple beings all human rights
As they go home to their bright lights
Talk about freedom to work and play
Perhaps they'll wake up one day

The Census man is coming to me

The census man is coming to me
Wonder why he didn't come when I was three
I waited and waited at the orphans gate
As they spun that dreadful web of fate
Left me behind with my sisters three
Poor dad and mum and families left us be
Played the game of war and took me away
Made us pawns in the wars of yesterday
And like now we didn't know what they did & do
After all these years it was all for revenue
Far more important as now to hide the facts
Under those horrible secrets acts
And I waited then and now I wait again
But now of course the difference is I have a brain
And ask why you are coming after all this time
For you didn't care for the victims of a nations crime
That killed and maimed millions and left behind
So many innocents from the ranks of mankind
As monsters roamed the world with their guns
Using gas and bombs mixed with our sons
And were so busy making millions as before
Taking lives everywhere to make up the score
Now you have the nerve to knock on my door
Saying open up for you know it's the law
For you only want to catch the ones who
Escape the net and evade revenue

15.5.1978

The common bond

Her face was pale and wan
Accentuated by the black dress she had on
Just like any other mother whose
Son was in prison and had everything to lose
Her face was creased and lined with fear
As the guards pushed she did not seem to hear
Their voices rough like their hearts of stone
Only could she think how to atone
For whatever it was her son had done
In Spain where being poor is a crime from which to run
So I took her hand and tried to say
My son too was in a very bad way
He too had fallen and placed too much
Faith in justice and found he was out of touch
With those he loved and held so dear
Finding he could no longer shed a tear
So I matched my steps with hers as we walked along
For not one word could I speak in her native tongue
And pressed her hand sharing a common bond
Then bade farewell as she passed beyond
I know not how or why or where
Only that we did but share one universal care
To reach out over all the world to the fond
Mothers regardless of language or creed in one common bond

The eyes of the night

They watched me as I walked along
The eyes of the night and I heard their song
Lights appeared in the houses one by one
Then I knew that day was done
A bullfrog croaked in the stream by my side
Fireflies danced just like a bride
Cars rushed by with eyes so bright
Piercing thru the shades of night
Leaves rustled as the rising wind sighed
It spoke out loud then slowly died
And the owl looked out and said twit twoo
The eyes of the night watched as I grew
Uneasy and hastened my footsteps to go home
Vowing no more in the darkness to roam
My heart beat swiftly as bats flew close
And the thoughts in my mind made me almost morose
The birds in the tree fell quiet except
For the nightingale as he kept
Me enthralled that such a small thing
Could fill my heart and make it sing
The eyes of the night crept into my heart
Like cupid threw that well known dart
Crickets disturbed my thoughts as I passed
Dogs started barking as I hurried so fast
All was noise and peace had gone
Bells rang out ding dong ding dong
Eyes of the night watched as I hurried inside
Sounds faded and just died
I was surrounded by friends in the New England town
Worth more than a ransom or a king's crown

West Springfield, Mass., USA, 4.7.1980

The first rose

The first rose as it blooms each year
Brings to my eyes the glimmer of a tear
Primroses and violets too whose
Perfumes will never never lose
Their charms for again each year
They like the birds will reappear
And even if they arrive late
Bring such colour they seem to know the date
And if that rose should ever vanish
The singing in my heart would stop and banish
Selfish greed making hate and war
Misery and killing and what for
As I look into the heart of the rose
And hope that never will we lose
Sight of that beauty with a tear in my eyes
As the first rose blooms under the skies

27.12.1975

The flag of peace

The chestnut trees in Regents Park
Were put there it seems just for the lark
And as you walk by the Regents Canal
You can hear someone calling to his pal
For living here so many years
And having shed so many tears
When the children were very young
And life for them had only just begun
Always remembering the peace and tranquillity
When unable to cope with any disability
Rushing to the park to drown the sorrow
Or maybe just to think or wallow
In self pity or to align thoughts in tune
To the songs of the birds for there's plenty of room
For all to share even at the hour
When folk pour from offices whilst waiting for the shower
To subside or to bask in the sunshine and pine
Thinking that even the Birch and the Lyme
The Sparrow, the Dove, the Lark and each living thing
Depend on each other to help and to bring
Pleasure, peace and hope of a better world
Under which ever flag of allegiance is unfurled

The four leaf clover

I searched the whole world over
And at last I found a four leaf clover
Carefully I pressed it in the pages of a book
And each day I opened it to have another look
Just to see if it was still there, and I wished
My thoughts ran riot as I made my list
The four leaf clover I ask is it true
That our dreams will come to pass & too
Will old father time wait for our kids to grow
Or will our leaders destroy them, do you know
Oh please can you take away poverty and war
Give us the good old fashioned law
The law of gravity that puts us on top
Can you give us enough make the greedy stop
Hurting our children as they take everything away
So slowly no one knows till it's gone one day
Oh please now I've found you I wish I wish every day
Don't let them I beg you take their lives and happiness away

The footsteps I left in the sand

I left my footsteps in the sand
As I flew back to my troubled land
And they'll still be there in future days
In the brilliant sun and massive waves
And here I sit and still hear the cries
Of birds as the echo of the day fades and dies
I look up at the endless blue of the sky
Hear the whisper of the clouds flying high
I watch the sparrows as they come near
Ask them where do you come from ol' dear
But there's no answer only the wind in my ear
As I leave my footprints in the sand
And a piece of my heart, as well as my hand
Outstretched and filled with love and peace to hold
The hearts of humanity for I care not for gold
And I left behind too, a piece of my heart
To give to my darlings from whom I part
As the world says our rulers, prospers and grows
The pearls so precious and who knows
As the great river just flows and flows
For one day they'll leave their footprints in the sand
As a little piece of my heart echoes over the land

The guiding hand

You are always in my mind
Always you are good and kind
Thinking only to do your best
And watching o'er us without rest
I feel your gentle kindly hand
Guiding me across the land
Oh my lord do not sigh
Or flutter or pass me by
For we'll meet perhaps by chance
Maybe to exchange a glance
Full of joy and happiness
Beauteous as a child's caress
For what transpires far far behind
The corners of my busy mind
With human frailties we all share
You help us all in trouble and in care
By being good and oh so kind
Staying always in mind
With your gentle hand
Guiding us across the land

The little lost soul

The little boy who died so tragically I fear
Unwanted and unloved with no one near
He never spoke for who was there
To shed a tear or help or hear
His cries for from birth it seemed that he
Was not meant to have or to be
One of the great human race
For no one looked with love upon his face
So at last he slipped away to the land
Of the never never band
There to await the reunion of his little soul
For he never never did achieve his goal
That poor poor tragic darling babe
In his little lonely grave

The Moon went down just like that

The sun followed me all the way
Every time I looked up it wouldn't go away
It shone and shone all the way on me
It picked me out especially
Then at last he got tired and said
I've had enough and went to bed
Trees and fields and roads and soon
They grew dark and up popped the moon
And that followed me again
Thank goodness it didn't rain
White Cliffs of Dover fell down to the sea
And then the moon followed me
On the ship as it sailed away
To that town they call Calais
I thought of my children and my eyes
Clouded a little and the skies
Still looked down didn't care
So cloudless covered everywhere
I never forget them, go away tears
And all those wars and the fears
All those loved ones who went to war
Even tho' most of them I never saw
And my grandchildren who every day
Come by and my mind was far away
Then suddenly the moon went down in the sky
Disappeared just like that, I wonder why

29.9.1985

The orphan

There once was an orphan who
Was left on a doorstep to coo
And laugh her way alone through life
Little knowing that poverty was rife
So no one could afford to keep this mite
And several attempts were made alright
To give her away and hope would fade
For some unknown reason she never stayed
As folk grew weary and sent her back
Little knowing she would get a whack
If she made a little fuss
Or made her clothes and hair in a muss
Then there were the floors to scrub
And if she failed there was a great hubbub
So to the dormitory she was sent
With bread and water and to repent
For being such a wicked so-and-so and
Was told how god was over all the land
So stop being wicked and think how lucky you are
For wherever you go whether near or far
Show how grateful you are and go down on your knees
And thank god you are alive and say please
And that you will always strive
To be good and patient not to deride
Your betters as you are only an orphan
So just live and forget how it all began

The pinewood box

The politicians are wicked it seems
As they invade our privacy and our dreams
With smiles that fill our hearts with dread
While they put up the price of our bread
Insidiously they tell us it's for your own good
That they put up the price of homes and food
As they relax in their mansions they're alright jack
But one of these days they'll get it back
Then they'll run just like the poor fox
Hunted to the end in a pinewood box
For they cannot evade the fate which will come
And what they've done to everyone
By taking away the laughter and fun
From the eyes of our families by the things they've done
The wars and the horror they think we forget
And still not content have the exocet
Gloat over radiation and sell water too
Oil, coal, education, and the old who never knew
For alas as children they never grew
With that wonderful family that was taken away
They had no pinewood boxes or money to pay
But the rulers have always had their way
Preferred wars and killing as they do today

20.12.1967

The price of life

The price of life is more than gold
A babe the young and even old
For one life lost thru' the years
Erupts into the vale of tears
Oh peace why do you fly away
Into space why don't you stay
Speak to us then you can go
To where the sea and rivers flow
Touch the hearts of everyone
With the kiss of a child then run
Take away the gun bombs and horror
From the faces of our children give them back tomorrow
Turn off those celestial lights
And put on those human rights
Take away those weapons and things
Instead of deprivation give them wings
Of love peace plenty for it costs nothing at all
To send our Cinderella to the ball
Send us back a Robin Hood
Bring our babes back from the wood
Give them homes and food fit for a king
Let them play and let them sing
For hunger and deprivation breeds
Violence for the human body needs
Food for minds they know well
For they make wars those who sell
Weapons missiles and the guns
To the highest bidder in exchange for sons
And families of the poor who have no means
To protest or indulge in endless dreams
Tho' rich or poor the price of young or old
Is still far beyond the price of gold

The protest

Yes, yes I will protest
In spite of all and with great zest
Even if the powers that be
Rain blows upon me ceaselessly
I will shout both loud and long
If I think that they are wrong
As all we want is a pleasant life
Free from worry and from strife
So yes, yes, I will protest

As down the ages my voices will go
So that future generations will know
That it's for them we fight
For the freedom to choose what's right
To march with heads held high
With goodness and kindness to get us by
And I will say to each of you
We love you truly, truly we do
But still I will protest
Both loud and long and with great zest

11.11.1974

The Protest, Lyrics Irene Romilly 1974,
song created and performed by Mimi, February 2009, © 2014, available from mimi-uk.com

The rainbow

We struggle to find the pot of gold
And see a notice which says it's sold
Looking into the crystal ball
Listening intently to hear the call
I see a rainbow in the sky
It turns and bends as it passes by
Then someone shouts for we've struck oil
There's a concerted rush to reach the soil
I dig deeper and deeper and I find
That I'm going slowly out of my mind
In the end I close my eyes
Dreaming dreaming of all those goodbyes
Awaking from my slumberland
Following the ever outstretched hand
Straining my eyes I search the skies
Thro' the mist to the sunrise
Treading softly I look down and see
Diamonds galore and all for me
Then I know it's all a dream
But wake me gently so I'll not scream
For I know there are no diamonds there
And can only sit and stare
As I wait for the phone to ring
Wishing wishing that I like a king
Could order the creditors to be gone
For they are part of a great big con

30.5.1967

The rising tide

Oh! Stop this terrible talk of war
Not only does it kill the poor
By the simple expedient of murder by law
Of all those innocent lives, I ask what for?
And still nobody ever asks why
Our rulers start wars, and make us cry
Those politicians, who don't care a jot
It's always been like that since the year dot
And we can't hit back 'cause if we do
There's always wars and prisons to get rid of you
And then up comes that rising tide
To destroy us before it can subside
Bringing destruction and oblivion worldwide
That hurts us all whichever side

The thief of time

I'm walking along with the blues
Not nails in hands and feet, but in my shoes
Hunger in my heart, body and my mind
Being a thief, a thief of time
Half of my mind goes on and on
Talking and talking and then they're gone
Leaving behind those that never die
Only propagate their species, pass on by
Taking possession of those who lack fire
And everything the human brain can desire
For I am a thief, a thief of time
I want to give it back in rhyme
And tho' I live forever until that Domesday Book
Closes upon the scene just took
The law in their hands, caught up with fear
Making laughter instead of a tear
Stop them dying from the neck down
Left behind, tragically alive like a clown
Leaving faint hearts to start all over again
Saying you can't take it with you, so it's all the same
Pack up and go gracefully, don't shout
For the sand, the sand is running out
I'm a thief, I'm a thief of time

30.5.1967

There's no such thing as democracy

Raise your glasses raise them high
Promise the earth, sea and sky
An election's coming and we've nearly won
For we won't tell anyone what we've done
Smile just smile, as you say
Inflation and cuts have had their way
Secretly aim the atoms to blow us away
Leave behind the dust of yesterday
Crush them just like you did the flower
Of our men on the poppy fields make us cower
Brainwash the masses say they can't win
Of course they can't good old Dusty Bin
Wave the flag that Union Jack
March to their music don't come back
Pay your taxes for you know
No one gets anything back oh no
Try just try to win and you'll see
There's no such thing as democracy

11.11.1985

They forget I fear

It's not at the time you feel the loss
But as you grow just like the moss
You go through life and do not feel
How much control is held by the wheel
For our names are stamped on the band
Of our clothes as we stand
Confused and helpless as we pass
From babyhood to a higher class
And do not know that when they say
You're an orphan so get out of the way
That this will be the theme of life
Which has been brought about by strife
So it's not at the time you feel the loss
Of all the things just like you toss
A coin and then kick it aside
For life is one long long ride
You try so hard when people come
Looking appraisingly as the sun
Goes down for we don't want you today
So go back to your life and play
And remember all those who die
But forget the ones who are left to sigh
As all alone with parents gone
Darkness has fallen and there is no song
As we walk around with hands outstretched
Begging for love, is it so far-fetched

6.11.1970

They forget the rainbow has an end

Take it, take it, take it away
That horror, those weapons, don't bring them back today
Tomorrow and forever, please please please
Give them to the monsters that live in the seas
Bury them down down and down
Take away that aura and myth that they constitute a crown
Take away those minds that create such things
For the glorification of queens and kings
Put them back in the mountains from whence they came
Make all those Gods realise their shame
As they pray in the churches, praise those who gain
As they laud those who make millions just for a game
Taking more than their fair share they never stop
Grumble about the state of the world they sit on top
Of a rainbow but they forget it has an end
Thunder and lightning just round the bend
But they always forget retribution not to god or anyone
Only to humanity and all under the sun
The flowers trees animals and more important than all
Is the flower of the earth the ones who down the ages call
Raise their voices above the Babel created by greed
Those wonderful humans who are the brunt of a deadly deed
But one day we mustn't make it too late
We have to speak up and do something old mate
Before the weapons and poison of our race
Will pervade the atmosphere and even space
And we won't hear our children cry out for milk or even bread
For without exception even they will be dead

5.10.1984

They gave us a sign, leave us alone, we'll be fine

They gave a sign those elements
As they turned the earth into sediments
And I believe they gave a sign
That said take your hands away we're fine
As the earth and sky was rent
With the most terrible sound as it gave vent
To that creeping fear as the dark
Came down over Noah's ark
And there'll be no animals or a human race
And like Canute who couldn't stop the tide or the face
Of the earth and sky with his power
And like our rulers wanted to make us cower
As they play that age-old game
Of who is who and what's your name
They can't see that the elements have the last word
Can flood the universe bringing havoc to man or bird
So make the earth sea and sky
All for one and all who cannot buy
As the skies erupt and give a sign
Telling everyone share and everything will be fine
If only you all just take what you need
Whatever race colour or even creed

They never learn

I watch our rulers and not one of them cares
For they're all right jack and can go anywhere
Well fed housed and not a single thought
Of anyone else as they shrug and say they ought
To cut cut cut stop the brains and the hands of the ones
Who've slaved to give those monsters guns
With which to kill all the surplus by desecrating their sons
Prosper and say we're alive and well fed
Who cares if the lower classes are dead
Tighten your belts but what do they do
They look like human beings that's perfectly true
They go all over and shake hands
With everyone in all other lands
Pretending they're interested singing their favourite song
Or an anthem to save behave like King Kong
But one day there'll be no food brought to their doors
For they can't see humanity is beyond the laws
And I say to them why don't you tell what they did to our men
When they were in France for no one remembered when
Our soldiers were massacred and shot like dogs instead
Of bringing them back home they preferred them dead
They hushed it all up like they do today
It mattered not for they forget one day
That robots and computers will turn a deaf ear
They won't be so easy to control or fill with fear
And if I can see I'll almost feel sorry for their plight
The dilemma they created for the poor will like the night
Enfold them for they even have to dig their own graves
For they will have destroyed all the poor slaves
So they won't be able to say we won't turn
For they'll know it's too late for them to learn

They say

The Christians they say are fighting the Jews
Arabs and Asians all with the Blues
Fighting and killing just like bears
For what they say is rightfully theirs
They open their mouths and what comes out
Peace peace peace they all shout
And instead of trying as they should
To help one another if they only would
All we can do is watch and say
Give them hearts not made of stone or clay
For the land will be here when they go away
So make them look at the earth and the sun
So no one will kill or raise a gun
Or fight against their brothers whatever race
And remain together in one place
Christians Jews any nationality at all
Living in peace until that last call
And let equality raise its head
For there's plenty for all in spite of what's been said

8.8.1985

They should have chosen equality

I listen to those bods talking such rot
Get rid of some weapons they say, I say get rid of the lot
Maggie and Ronnie and the Russian, can't spell his name
What about us for we all take the blame
I'm waiting for our capitalists what lovely people they are
To put in a tender for that moon and star
And I hear all these old men and women spout
About all those wicked common bods getting their fingers out
And how many crawlers who clap their hands
Realise what they're condoning in all lands
It won't only be me or you who'll go
It'll be everyone even prince and pauper you know
It takes one finger and a few seconds in time
Then they needn't worry about combating crime
And do they think anyone will be there
Except of course those in bunkers everywhere
Picking out the most important ones who
Have made millions out of you know who
And I don't care if they're worried for they'll have time to reflect
Look around and see the results of that Exocet
Then try to get back to the world outside maybe
And the most important race they killed to be free
And the greed that fills their eyes now will disappear
When there's no one to pander or crawl or speak up against nuclear
For that's the thing you can't play with no way
For it will hit you back and there's nothing to say
You've had it old chum and you don't even know
What if anything will be left anyway, so
There's no retribution or acceptance for no one will win
And there's no money, gold, shares, monopolies or any single thing
And all the talk and all the promises I know well
Will culminate in the road to hell

They will lie

There he lies in a soldier's grave
Like millions of others I'm told who gave
Their lives so that we could all be free
And still - still we cannot see
That violence never pays, even though
Waves may come, and tides may go
We raise our hands to brandish a gun
At the least misdemeanour under the sun
We forget the soldiers in their graves
Who fought and died even for the knaves
For it seems to me their heads are full
Of emptiness and they play the fool
And they know one day that they will lie
Under the earth and open sky
Our tears fall fast as we think how they die
So lonely and forgotten as they pass by

6.10.1974

This heart just broke

Long long ago when in my teens
This heart just broke and smashed to smithereens
The pieces made a pattern of sorrow
Until love came beckoning to follow
Then at last it began to mend
As spring came making trees sway and bend
Giving way to long summer days
Gradually fading bringing the haze
Of autumn as all the leaves fall dying
And alone with a broken heart crying
Oh so long long long ago
Until at last tears cease to flow
Cease cease to flow and bringing
Peace and love and sweet singing
Those voices from long long ago
In the days before I loved you so

Those old Gods

From the days of Adam and Eve
It's what I heard and I believe
They used fig leaves and an apple then
Cain and Abel and Noah's ark when
Two of each animal went down in the ark
Then up popped those minds up for a lark
Let's bring in a myth and pray
We'll call it god and we're on our way
Let's pretend even though
There's nowhere the increments can go
Nowhere to go but down here you know
And all the time from the year dot
Those old gods they take the lot

6.11.1988

Time

Time creeps inexorably on
Making us wonder where it has gone
Leaving behind all of our friends
And changing the outlook and the trends
Of modern behaviour, replacing the old
Friendliness and beauty, for the cold
Apathy of the appraising eye
Of another generation passing us by
And all we can do is to wish
On the moon and hope that the dish
Will not run too quickly away with the spoon

Irene's relative, Roget (of Roget's Thesaurus fame), also wrote a poem about time.

Time wastes us all

Time wastes us all
Our bodies and our wits
But we waste time
So time and us are quits

Peter Mark Roget, 1779-1869

Today is yesterday and now it's tomorrow

I woke up and now it's tomorrow
And today is now yesterday I realise with horror
Turn on the radio must be careful you see
Only one small coin between darkness and me
I turn on the telly silly old me to hear and see
All the big bods talking about you and me
How we might if we're here get eighty pence
That's for around fifty years slavery our increments
Turn it over there's football and snooker oh no
Then I tune in on the radio
Make sure you all stay with me
Says a bright voice can't help it for you see
Unless which is likely the fifty pence 'P'
Goes out we're committed to put up with it for you know
There's nothing else to do there's nowhere to go
A minister resigns who cares as all the poor things
Hear about all the wicked countries and their sins
Spies and terrorists and I laugh thru' my tears
What can I get for my grandchildren poor dears
The shops are getting up their yearly campaign
For that awful festival I think they're insane
For now they've even priced the kids out and us
Of everything worthwhile can't even ride a bus
Or talk to them on the telephone
As I sit there in my cold basement home
Where I wait and wait for my pittance to come
Just a few pounds that are the price of dads and mum

Today or yesterday

They're coming they're coming to take me away
Was it today I can't remember or yesterday
I wonder for I forget what I have done
For there's nothing to steal and no prize to be won
No food in the cupboard so it can't be that
I wish I could remember oh dash and drat
A knock on the door oh let me in to cut
Off your electricity for you cannot pay us but
I stutter and stammer and think of the years
Of hunger and poverty and fight back the tears
Oh I wish I could remember as I sit and grow old
How the bill was so high oh, I'm so cold
And I cannot remember if it was tomorrow or today
Or maybe they said they'd come yesterday
As I sit and wait to see if they come today
For they said they're coming to take me away
I wonder will there be food and some fun
Maybe television and heat and somewhere to run
Away from those monsters who knock on the door
To lock me up for my crime is being old and poor
Oh I wish I could remember was it today
Or even tomorrow or maybe it was yesterday

23.3.1981

Uncle Sam

The soldiers and folk in Vietnam
Are vainly waiting for their Uncle Sam
To say the word that means so much
For they are slowly losing touch
To become the faceless ones
For all they can hear are the drones
Of planes and bombs and boom of guns
Amid the hovering figures of nuns
As children cry and long for bed
And the sky becomes an angry stormy red
Hurrying along vainly trying
To stifle their fear of dying
Oh how wicked we have become when innocent babes
Are driven slowly into early graves
While peacemakers drive to their plush
Hotels wining and dining to make us blush
As they laugh and chatter to each other gaily
Forgetting the hundreds who are dying daily
As unthinkingly they all leave
Talk of peace for another fateful eve
So wake up wake up Uncle Sam and play
Santa Claus if only just for a day
For surely this really is a must
To help you to sleep the long sleep of the just

Water water everywhere

Water water everywhere and not a drop to drink
How can they say who has or has not water then I think
And wonder if there is a god who's up there looking down
On all those people who, live outside the town
And it makes me feel, well and truly quite dumbstruck
Finding it hard to believe that lack of power or a buck
Pound cent or dollar, could bring this all about
As deprivation increases and I want so much to shout
How dare they take the resources of the earth away from those
Who by a cruel twist of fate can't access the water as it flows
Making lives so miserable that the masses cry
And the rulers in control start to clamp down by
Taking 90 percent of the water to use for their own
They cannot see the hatred and resentment that they've sown
Then I see how they pray to the great super being
Loudly exhorting as all they seem to be seeing
Are the well chosen ones who are of their own faith and creed
But surely humanity of any religion is beyond such hate and greed
Food water shelter is surely the right of all
Whether Jew or Gentile, black, white, large or small
And I can hear their voices all echoing around
As I watch and see, so much water on the ground
Running away into the sea, and then lost
Such a precious commodity at such a terrible cost
For in my mind religion is a two-edged sword
Causing bloodshed and horror at the command of a word
And I wish I had the power to make it a crime
Forever down the ages and for all time
To take away water and resources and what's more
Tormenting those who have nothing or are poor
And to fight over land which we've all done down the ages
Or make any excuse worshipping the dead and getting in rages

For whatever they say about those who are dead
It's the living who are here and must be watered and fed
So who has the right to say to any person, son or daughter
What section of society can or cannot have water
For there's plenty for all, water water everywhere
And more than enough and plenty more to share

We fought in the Wars

We fought in the wars
And kept all the laws
Hid under the ground
And on top without a sound
Time passed so quickly and they said we were free
Passed by as our own were like the Pharisee
Vote they said so everyone who's got
Can still be in the rat race for the lot
Sit down and be quiet
Don't forget three's a riot
Take your pittance and stand
Like all good Britons in the land
Start working now so you can
Contribute to the extinction of the common man

1.7.1989

We free

The earth is free and the skies are free
And so is the air but why not we
They come and say if you don't pay
We'll put you away until judgement day
And don't you dare to walk on the grass
Or jump or skip or attempt to pass
A derogatory remark for on your head will fall
The wrath of the lord and life begins to pall
And your mind is confused as they try to spoil
The pleasures of life and your mind will recoil
As you think this is not just a passing phase
As the hours pass into days and days

What is the Hon. Lady having to eat today

What, I ask, is the Honourable Lady having to eat today?
I'll bet anything she doesn't say
Scotts' porridge oats is a winner
And you can have it for breakfast, tea and dinner
Tho' Scott of the Antarctic was great
Scott's porridge oats is better old mate

What may I ask have we done to you

What may I ask, have we done to you
That all you do is destroy us too
Just as you did in the First World War
Took away all our families what for
Then you took our mums and the rest
Now we've learned as you do your best
To leave us to suffer from cold and soft soap
I realise now that there is no hope
And I wonder what crime we committed long ago
That when we're old and British our rulers show
The utmost unconcern as to our fate
With absolutely no rebate
And debt collectors at the door
Ask myself what crime I committed against the law

30.5.1985

Whatever happened to Robin Hood

Oh whatever happened to Robin Hood
Who roamed around doing such good
For the poor and the downtrodden
And all the ones who are forgotten
He robbed the rich to feed the poor
As he rode around the forest and moor
He was so good so very good
That man who was called Robin Hood
For nowadays they close their eyes
Ignoring all the hopeless cries
For they're so busy wanting to be
Rich and famous they cannot see
All the misery for their greed
Is to wine and dine and feed
To ride in comfort across the land
And then to their houses, large and grand
All they want is to reach the top
And they know not where to stop
Oh where is Robin Hood today
Why oh why did he go away
For the man who did such good
And his name was Robin Hood
Who robbed the rich to feed the poor
Roaming roaming over forest and moor
Oh come back come back Robin Hood
We need you so much to do more good

30.5.1970

Where the primroses grow

I want so much to go where the primroses grow
But I know I cannot get my steps to go
For my heart is weak and my mind
Confused and it is such a bind
To go to where the yellow primroses grow and
Your voice in my head and your hand
In mine makes my heart beat like a drum
And I pray love will stay as I look for a crumb
Of affection tho' I know love has gone
But I still carry on and on and on
With hope in my heart that we'll never part
Even if we live forever as my faint heart
Goes wearily to where the primroses grow
And even if there is no glow I know
That when love is gone the voice in my head
Will always be there till I'm dead
Saying go go go, go do go
To the place where the yellow primroses grow

9.3.1964

Who will weep

Oh who will weep when we are gone
And the sun shines on and on
Oh who, oh who, will pay the band
For all those who like the sand
Are shifting and toiling all the while
Like the turbulent waters of the Nile
Oh who, oh who, remembers when
Our spirits rose as we wielded the pen
As fate dealt her many wiles
Casting us aside hiding her smiles
Slowing down as we lose the power
To subside gently like the shower
So who, oh who, will weep when we are gone
Leaving behind only the echo of a song
As we rock so slowly in the cradle deep
Taking refuge in tears, as we weep and weep

Winners or losers

Money always wins it's true
And stays down here whatever you do
Wisdom comes too late I fear
Never catches up till we're no longer here

You can't buy a river

Stepping on to my balcony my windows open wide
As I gaze upon the beauteous sea and tide
I see the almond blossom trees now in their fullest bloom
Which immediately banishes all my worldly gloom
Making me think how lucky that I can smile
Saying an inward prayer for the things in life worthwhile
For hark at the bird songs filling the air
And a lark calls to his mate for he has no care
For it seems they know that the bees and their honey
Exceed even the treasures that come with money
And alas how many of us stop to think
If we could help a precious child or give a drink
Of cool clear water or even make a river
A mountain stream or a wind to make you shiver
But care only for material gain not the wonders of life
Falling over each other to buy instruments of strife
Killing all the wonderful things that abound
Forgetting in their haste even to look around
At the beauties of earth and the sky
We could never never make them however much we try

19.12.1974

You have the right to buy

On the fourth I'm told I go to court
Silly woman I've been caught
Fifteen years ago they said
Sit down ol' age 'P' and be dead
But make sure that you can pay
For taxes rent gas light water and they say
Food and clothes and burials too
Jump when we tell you what to do
Don't ever say derogatory things
About wars, or Maastricht or any jolly thing
If you can't cope so they say
Call in help but you must pay
VAT on everything anyway
Revenue revenue all the way
What 'orrible years and decades too
I wonder what ever they're going to do
When all of that food starts to run out
And they imprison that very last ol' lout
And I look around at the streets and think
Why do they and the drains all stink
And fumes from the billion cars pollute
Causing sickness and cancer which they refute
And I see all the cars at a future date
Sitting there as they wait and wait
For a driver who you know will die
And where will they go without them and I sigh
Hear our rulers say you have the right to buy
Lucky you, you common ordinary guy

1.11.1992

You sent them to die

I look at them and I cry
How could they be heroes when they sent them to die
Or if they come back present them with a medal
Mind and body destroyed in a chair with a pedal
How can they look us in the eye
And go back to living in standards so high
Look at the ones to their eternal shame
Who signed away lives and made them take the blame
As the hoi polloi buy a dozen hats
Politicians monarchs lords blind as bats
They forget those very far away graves
For whom they say were the braves
Buried in secret till survivors said
Whatever happened to their dead
Sixty years after the next war came
And once again the elite made claim
To the ones they said were heroes who fell
Then hushed it up again and said they couldn't tell
For a hundred years for alas dead men tell no tales
Buy up everything stocks shares and sales
And they live in luxury and just like kings
Don't care if the poor have no homes and things
Saying they owe allegiance to this land
Take away what they slaved for to pay the band
And I wonder how they sleep as old soldiers die
Or come back minus leg arm or eye
You say they're heroes, give them medals and cry
Crocodile tears for you sent them to die

6.11.1979

You will you won't

You say you'll give me everything
Riches and fortune fit for a king
You say you will, you won't, you will
Until I've just about had my fill
For you cannot give me the sky and earth
I've seen and trod from the day of my birth
Nor can you give me love sincere
As you and I both know and fear
For there's a void in your heart
Stretching into the depths setting us apart
And I do not hear as you say again
How much you will give but only the pain
Remains for though you say over and over
You mean what you say, you cannot cover
The greed in your eyes and your heart
So I'll never never become a part
Of your life even if, you say you'll give me your all
For pride comes before a very big fall
And you cannot give me anything indeed
As the earth and sky are everything I need

Youth and age

I hear the sound of running feet
And then the voices oh so sweet
Of little children as they speak
Above the din and then comes a shriek
From the little girl who's seen a cat
And in her mind she's thinking that
It's the one she lost when she was two
But now she's nearly four and too
Is growing lovelier every day
As her brother rushes up to kiss
His nan for he is nearly six
And their minds are so clear
For they know who they hold dear

1971

Summary of *Take Me Oh Take Me*

The King's Cross bomb (possibly Argyle Street, 9th Sept 1940).

In 1940, Irene and her partner, Ali Mohammed Gulam shad, were staying in King's Cross with their son Nick (Niyaz, b.1937).

Irene said that this bomb fell in Argyle Street King's Cross, being a full moon it was a very clear night, and consequently very light. Apparently, the woman in the poem had gone out to get fish and chips for her husband and children (who were all on leave), whilst she was gone, the bomb fell and pierced a gas main, leaving the husband and their children trapped in the basement, slowly being gassed to death. Their screams could clearly be heard by everyone, but nobody could help them.

When the woman returned and realised what had happened, she pleaded hysterically *Take Me, Oh Take Me*, meaning her instead of her family. Meanwhile, the young Irene, clutching her infant son, surveyed the scene with horror.

Irene's son Nick would have been about three at the time, later, along with his brother Alan (Azad, b.1943) attended Argyle School, in King's Cross. Nick became a professor of maths at Leeds University and Alan, who died in 1984, a poet. See *Camden History Revue vol 20, pp 8, col. 3*, re; Irene's relationship with Gulam.

During the war, Irene moved to Heath Street, Hampstead and used the Tube station for shelter. Hampstead was much safer from bombs than King's Cross and she said it was easy to get properties there because people with money had fled and didn't want them.

It was from Heath Street that Ali Mohammed Gulam ran off, taking his two sons away from Irene. However, she found out where they were living in Hornsey several years later and kidnapped them back.

Summary of *My Heart is a Bird*

I believe that Irene was staying with her partner and two sons in Regents Sq, King's Cross, at the home of the elderly judge Dara (an Indian judge) when these bombs dropped circa 1943.

She said that she had ran out of the house with her two young sons and that a doodlebug had landed on the doorstep (not sure whether she meant literally). She had been knitting an outfit for her baby son Alan (Azad) then suddenly realised that she had left her wool behind. Without thinking, she rushed back to retrieve it and luckily for her, the doodlebug did not explode!

Irene's last campaign

...But the council wasn't her only bug bear. She was prominent in the local anti-poll tax campaign and according to one friend, she would often picket the offices of national newspapers and *"berate them for telling lies."*

Her anarchistic poems attacked the rich ruling elite while thousands of people, herself included, lived in poverty...

excerpt taken from Irene Romilly Obituary, Camden New Journal, September 15 1994

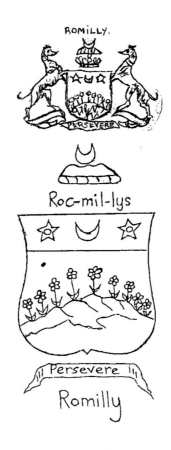